The Metrical Life of
St. Robert of Knaresborough

EARLY ENGLISH TEXT SOCIETY

Original Series, No. 228

1953 (for 1947), reprinted 1968

PRICE 40s.

Ipe precatur willmi nemani a Roberto

To Robert Holon where þat he
befor þe fott fell on hys kne
And sayd Robert forgeff my all
my grevouns gyltes : And I sall
Robert forgaff and willam kyssed
And blythely veryly þe hand þam klyssed

To Grymbalde Kyrk stans gyff I the [hic dedit Ro-
land this lytyll all þat payd ysell   berto possessio-
þe tyst pyt on the est veyse   nes elimosina
Swetly here twey opon I the gyse
halfe and half gofe deghtes lyffe
Sweetly ley I grauntte the of my gre
To all the porsioner of thi place
Also sustinamce I sall the fend
ffay pole day pyll a zere to thend
Off dayse throtton folowand
Oyn þat I lyff in this land
A mese dayse of flesshe and fysshe
for thretton men satt they now mysse
One messe mast yet be of impote
ffaty chastee conquorors and amoste
he come the goddott where he cambe
off a low mikke a lambe
he made how mikke yat Robert mened
and made how wassow in this world

The Metrical Life of St. Robert of Knaresborough

TOGETHER WITH THE
OTHER MIDDLE ENGLISH PIECES
IN BRITISH MUSEUM MS.
EGERTON 3143

EDITED BY
JOYCE BAZIRE

Published for
THE EARLY ENGLISH TEXT SOCIETY
by
OXFORD UNIVERSITY PRESS
LONDON   NEW YORK   TORONTO

OXFORD
UNIVERSITY PRESS

Great Clarendon Street, Oxford OX2 6DP
United Kingdom

Oxford University Press is a department of the University of Oxford.
It furthers the University's objective of excellence in research, scholarship,
and education by publishing worldwide. Oxford is a registered trade mark of
Oxford University Press in the UK and in certain other countries

© The Early English Text Society 1953

The moral rights of the authors have been asserted

Database right Oxford University Press (maker)

First Edition published in 1953
Reprinted 1968

All rights reserved. No part of this publication may be reproduced,
stored in a retrieval system, or transmitted, in any form or by any means,
without the prior permission in writing of Oxford University Press,
or as expressly permitted by law, or under terms agreed with the appropriate
reprographics rights organization. Enquiries concerning reproduction
outside the scope of the above should be sent to the Rights Department,
Oxford University Press, at the address above

You must not circulate this book in any other form
and you must impose this same condition on any acquirer

Published in the United States of America by Oxford University Press
198 Madison Avenue, New York, NY 10016, United States of America

British Library Cataloguing in Publication Data
Data available

Library of Congress Cataloging in Publication Data
Data available

Original Series, 228

ISBN 978-0-19-722228-7

TO MY

FATHER AND MOTHER

ADDENDA
1968

FURTHER information concerning Trinitarian houses in Great Britain and Ireland has been collected, in the light of which certain statements must be revised or added to, though sometimes the full significance still cannot be determined. References to the first edition of *St. Robert* are given in brackets.

(p. 19)   '... 1200'.[2] Ten other Trinitarian establishments in England followed that of Hounslow (though apparently not all were independent), only two of them, Knaresborough and Walknoll, Newcastle, being in northern England. Information is to be found concerning one in Ireland and eight in Scotland. Although references are made to separate Provincials for England and Scotland, the position of the Irish house in respect of a Provincial is at present unknown. One of the English Provincials whose names are recorded ...

(p. 23)   ... he was patron saint. There is no evidence to warrant the assumption that Robert was considered as patron saint at any other Trinitarian house in England, unless the fact that in 1286 certain proctors are described as being 'of the house of St. Robert of Knarsburgh and Oxford' (*Patent Rolls, 14 Ed. I*, m. 21 [1281-92, p. 224]) indicates this. (However, in the fourteenth century, after the Black Death, Oxford's connexion seems rather to have been with the house at Hounslow.) As is pointed out in the note to l. 30, other references in official documents to 'St. Robert's' are always to the house at Knaresborough.

(p. 24)   ... the only other northern English house of the Order,[1] though, since there was for some period a connexion with the house at Oxford, it is not impossible that a friar there of northern origin was the author. However, see p. 26, § 6.

(p. 100, note to l. 1183)   'President' is an unusual term to apply to the head of a Trinitarian house, 'minister' being the usual word. 'President' has, however, been found in a charter (cited by Henry Bourne in the Appendix to *The History of Newcastle upon Tyne* [Newcastle-upon-Tyne, 1736], granted when the Trinitarians were established at Walknoll in 1360. The official in charge of Walknoll is named as *custos* (warden), but the Minister of Knaresborough is to be President of the place and has certain supervisory duties. None the less it is difficult to determine whether or not the use of this term has any significance for identifying the author of the piece.

PREFACE

MY attention was first drawn to St. Robert of Knaresborough while I was a graduate student in the University of Leeds, when Professor Bruce Dickins suggested that I should undertake an edition of the 'Metrical Life'. Professor Dickins has ever since maintained an interest in the progress of the text and I am much indebted to him for the practical form this interest has taken.

No less is my debt to Mr. R. M. Wilson who has guided me in this work almost from the beginning and whose kindly encouragement and forthright criticism have always proved of inestimable value. The suggestions offered me, too, on many occasions by Professor S. Potter and Mr. A. C. Cawley have been much appreciated.

I am also most grateful to all those who have helped me by their advice and their interest in the preparation of this edition; more particularly would I mention here Mr. W. Beattie, Lieutenant-Colonel H. F. Chettle, Miss R. M. Clay, Mr. E. Colledge, the Reverend P. Grosjean, S.J., Chancellor F. Harrison, Professor D. Knowles, Dr. R. Offor, Professor H. Orton, Dr. D. Oschinsky, the Reverend Angelo Raine, Mr. G. B. Townend, Professor C. L. Wrenn, and Dr. C. E. Wright.

To the Trustees of the British Museum and to the Syndics of the University Library, Cambridge, I am obliged for photostats and permission to examine manuscripts.

JOYCE BAZIRE

LIVERPOOL
July 1951

CONTENTS

British Museum Ms. Egerton 3143, f. 49ᵛ *Frontispiece*

ABBREVIATIONS	x
INTRODUCTION	1
SELECT BIBLIOGRAPHY	40
TEXT	42
NOTES	82
SELECT GLOSSARY	101
APPENDIX A	113
APPENDIX B	129
APPENDIX C	134
APPENDIX D	144

ABBREVIATIONS

(For abbreviations of book-titles see also BIBLIOGRAPHY*)*

AME.	All the pieces in Middle English in the British Museum Manuscript, Egerton 3143, except *The Metrical Life of St. Robert of Knaresborough* (*M.*), i.e. *D.*, *O.*, *P.*, and *R.*
Angl.	Anglian.
Chron. Lan.	*Chronicon de Lanercost.*
D.	*De initio creacionis Ordinis Sancte Trinitatis* (pp. 72–76).
E.E.T.S.	Early English Text Society Publication.
Egert.	Latin prose life of St. Robert found in the British Museum Manuscript, Egerton 3143 (*Appendix A*—pp. 113–28).
EM.	East Midland.
Har.	Latin prose life of St. Robert found in the British Museum Manuscript, Harley 3775 (*Appendix B*—pp. 129–33).
HT.	*De innovatione Ordinis Sancte Trinitatis* (*Appendix D*—pp. 144–8).
LVL.	*De nobilitate vite Sancti Roberti confessoris* (*Appendix C*—pp. 134–44).
M.	*The Metrical Life of St. Robert of Knaresborough—De vita et conuersacione Sancti Roberti iuxta Knaresburgum* (pp. 42–72).
Nh.	Northumbrian.
Nthn.	Northern.
nonWS.	non-West Saxon.
O.	*Oracio Presidentis* (pp. 77–80).
P.	*A Prayer* (pp. 76–77).
R.	*Oracio ad beatum Robertum* (pp. 80–81).
WM.	West Midland.

INTRODUCTION

THE MANUSCRIPT

'The Metrical Life of St. Robert of Knaresborough' (M.) and the other metrical pieces in Middle English (AME.) are to be found in the British Museum Manuscript, Egerton 3143, ff. 35^v–38^v, 39^v–63^v. The manuscript contains a collection of material in prose and poetry dealing with the life and cult of St. Robert, and no copies of these works are known from other sources. On palaeographical grounds the manuscript has been dated by Dr. Cyril Wright of the Department of Manuscripts, British Museum, as late fifteenth century.

It contains the following pieces, of which numbers 23, 24, 26, 29, and 30 are in English, and the remainder in Latin.

1. ff. 1^r–7^v.

   'De nobilitate vite Sancti Roberti confess(oris).'
   'In excelsis Salvatori . . . Singillatim, "Amen." '
   A life of St. Robert in 116 stanzas of four lines each; there is alliteration within the lines, and the stanzas are to be taken in pairs to form the rhyming pattern: aaab cccb. This is printed below, pp. 134–44. Abb. LVL.

2. ff. 7^v–10^r.

   'De innovatione Ordinis Sancte Trinitatis.'
   'Hic et fundo digni ducis . . . "Amen", dicant omnia.'
   An account of the foundation of the Order of the Holy Trinity in 44 stanzas with alliteration; the rhymes are formed on the same pattern as above. This is printed below, pp. 144–8. Abb. HT.

3. ff. 10^v–11^r.

   'Matutine de Sancto Roberto ex devocionem dicende.'
   'Iam, Roberte, famulos hora matutina . . . Sic ut poli perfruer mira mansione.' 'Antiphona: Te laudamus.' 'Collecta: Mentibus nostris.' 'Antiphona: Pulsa et cetera.'
   Every prayer occupies four lines of verse, and all, except those for *nona hora* and *hora completorii*, are followed by the verses, &c., which follow the first prayer—a rhyming couplet, 'Te laudamus . . . a tormento tristi', four lines of prose, 'Mentibus nostris . . . herimo concupivit', and a rhyming couplet, 'Pulsa presta . . . vanitatis visum. Amen'. Internal rhyme is also found in many of the verse lines.

'Hora matutina'—this asks that Robert will listen to the prayer and help 'us'.

'Hora prima'—a prayer asking for Robert's intercession for the well-being of men.

'Hora tercia'—a prayer for the well-being of the speaker.

'Hora sexta'—the speaker prays that he may be saved from carnal sin.

'Hora nona'—this asks Robert to obtain nectar from the heavenly fountain that it may inspire 'us'.

'Hora vesperarum'—the speaker asks that he may be kept from sin.

'Hora completorii'—a prayer that Robert will direct the speaker in the contemplative life of a solitary.

The last verse sums up *has horas canonicas*, and asks that Robert will help the speaker to endure his life on earth so that he may come later to heaven.

4. f. 11r-v.

'Quinque gaudia beati Roberti.'
'Gaude, norma nove vite . . . Orbem per terrarum.'

Stanza 1. Robert is a pattern of life.
„ 2. He was pleasing to God.
„ 3. He praised God in his cave.
„ 4. He made stags work in the field.
„ 5. Robert shines like a candle in the dark.
„ 6. Will Robert therefore help his servants?

Two stanzas form the rhyming pattern, aab ccb, and there is a certain amount of alliteration.

5. f. 11v.

'Antiphona: O Roberte, precibus . . . celi coniungamur.'

A rhyming couplet with alliteration asking Robert to help 'us' that we may be joined to the company of the saints; it is followed at the side by 'Oremus' 'Oracio'.

6. f. 11v.

'Deus qui beatum Robertum . . . eius intercessione perpetuo delectati.'

A short prayer in four lines of prose asking God, who favoured Robert, to help 'us' too.

7. ff. 11v-12r.

'Quindecim gaudia beati Roberti.'
'Gaude, felix ac fecunde . . . presta parans gloriam.'

Stanza 1. Robert's good and happy life.
„ 2. He was visited by heavenly beings.

Introduction 3

Stanza 3. Through love of Christ he came to Knaresborough.
„ 4. His mother appeared to him in sleep.
„ 5. The matron gave him the chapel of St. Hild.
„ 6. He was robbed of bread and water by thieves.
„ 7. Through Christ an enemy was made a friend.
„ 8. He healed Yvo's broken foot.
„ 9. He tamed a wild cow.
„ 10. He healed a lame beggar.
„ 11. He asked King John to make a new ear of corn from nothing.
„ 12. He drove the stags from the corn and used them in his plough.
„ 13. He prophesied that monks of Fountains would come for his body.
„ 14. Robert has gone to heaven.
„ 15. He purifies his servants.
„ 16. Will Robert pray to God to bring 'us' to glory ?

The stanzas rhyme aab ccb, with two to make the pattern. All have some alliteration.

8. f. 12r.

'Versiculus: O Roberte, rogita ... sempiternitatis.'

Rhyming couplet with a little alliteration, asking Robert to pray God to give 'us' the joys of eternity; it is followed at the side by 'Oremus' 'Oracio'.

9. f. 12r-v.

'Deus qui nos ... per Dominum nostrum Jesum.'

A short prayer in six lines of prose asking God that through Robert and through meditation on his life 'we' may come to heaven.

10. ff. 12v–14r.

'De eodem.'

'Plaude, plausus patrie pudiciciarum ... "Amen", dicantt omnia metum sine fine. Amen.'

It describes the ways in which Robert has afforded and still does afford help to others, with a request that he will help the one who is praying. There are eighteen stanzas, rhyming aaaa. Apart from the last four lines, nearly every word begins with p, which makes the poem difficult to translate.

11. f. 14r-v.

'O Roberte, rogita regem racionis ... Sumens ad solacia supplico salvare. Amen.'

The first eight stanzas contain a prayer to Robert to assist all in Orders. He always tried to help others during his lifetime, and now he is removed from the distresses of the world. The last four stanzas are a prayer to God to save and help all, with particular reference to ministers of the Church; some titles are mentioned—abbots, rectors, &c. Each stanza contains four lines, rhyming aaaa; the first eight have alliteration throughout the stanza on one letter, so that all these stanzas in order spell *ROBERTUS*; the other four have line-by-line alliteration, though two or three lines may have the same running on.

12. ff. 15r–31v.

'Hic incipit prologus de vita Sancti Roberti . . . qui cum Patre et cetera.'

A life of St. Robert in prose, edited by P. Grosjean, 'Vitae S. Roberti Knaresburgensis' (*Analecta Bollandiana*, lvii. 375–400). Part of this is also printed below, pp. 113–28.

13. ff. 31v–32r.

'Oracio in honore Sancti Roberti confessoris Cristi.'

'O patrone clementissime, summe regis . . . per omnia secula seculorum. Amen.'

A prayer to Robert in 21 lines of prose to grant all virtues to those *in sancte professionis proposito*.

14. f. 32r–v.

'Oracio pro loc⟨i⟩ stabilitate et eius habita⟨to⟩ribus.'

'Domine Jesu Criste, qui elegisti locum istum . . . nos perducat per te Jesu Criste.'

A prayer in eighteen lines of prose to Christ for those in the house of which Robert is patron saint, that they may carry out their obligations properly.

15. f. 32v.

'Memoria de Sancto Roberto confessore.'

'O Roberte, pastor pie . . . Facias pervenire.'

A prayer to Robert to save the suppliants from suffering on earth and to guide them to the heavenly kingdom. Ten lines of verse in two stanzas, rhyming aaaab ccccb; there is some alliteration.

16. f. 32v.

'Versiculus: Pro nobis ora, Roberte, qualibet hora.' 'Oremus' 'Oracio'.

17. f. 32v.

'Beati Roberti confessoris . . . sociata gloriari.'

A short prayer to the Lord in three prose lines asking that through Robert the suppliants may come to glory.

Introduction 5

18. f. 33ʳ.

'Item de Sancto Roberto.'

'Salve, gemma confessorum . . . Presens post exilium.'

A prayer to Robert, who had pity on the sinful, to help 'us' to gain heaven. Ten lines of verse in two stanzas, rhyming aaaab ccccb.

19. f. 33ʳ.

'Ora pro nobis, beate Roberte, ut supra.' 'Oremus.'

20. f. 33ʳ.

'Pretende nobis, Domine, . . . promereri valeamus, per Cristum Dominum nostrum. Amen.'

A short prayer to God in three lines of prose asking His help on the intercession of Robert.

21. ff. 33ʳ–35ʳ.

'Item de Sancto Roberto.'

'Ave, pater et patrone . . . hoc presta in perpetuum. Amen.'

A prayer in 57 rhyming couplets by someone in Robert's house to that saint, asking him to make him virtuous in all his deeds and in his character so that he may go to the land of the blessed. Some line-by-line alliteration.

22. f. 35ʳ⁻ᵛ.

'Versus circa tumbam eius.'

'Huius si vite bonitatem scribere noscem . . . Aut sunt serrantes aut in fide titubantes.'

In 12 rhyming couplets, with the first half-lines also rhyming together; these tell of the wonderful deeds of Robert and discuss the writer's ability to recount them; examples are given of his acts of healing.

23. ff. 35ᵛ–37ᵛ.

'Oracio Presidentis.'

'Hayle! Saint Robert, a confessoure . . . Amen, Amen per charite.'

A prayer to Robert in 47 English rhyming couplets, asking for help in the ruling of the house, that the speaker may act as befits the head of the house and so merit eternal bliss. This is printed below, pp. 77–80. Abb. *O*.

24. ff. 37ᵛ–38ᵛ.

'Oracio ad beatum Robertum.'

'Hayle! heremete mast þat ys of myght . . . I beseke the grauntte me this. Amen.'

6 *Introduction*

A prayer to Robert in 29 English rhyming couplets asking him to help and save the suppliant that he may go to heaven. This is printed below, pp. 80–81. Abb. *R*.

25. ff. 38v–39r.

'Hic incepit deprecacio Sancti Roberti heremite.'
'Inmense et ineffabilis misericordie Sancte Roberte . . . per Cristum Dominum nostrum. Amen.'

A prayer to Robert in 22 lines of prose; a résumé of what he did in life. Will he therefore ask Christ to help his son to continue steadfast in his profession, and may he come to heaven at last?

26. ff. 39v–60v.

'De vita et conversacione Sancti Roberti iuxta Knaresburgum.'[1]
'Thou luffly Lord of ylkay lede . . . Amen, Amen, per charite.'

A life of St. Robert in 505 rhyming couplets in English. This is printed below, pp. 42–72. Abb. *M*.

27. f. 60v.

'Salve sancte pater . . . duc nos ad regna polorum.'
Three lines in rhyming verse praising Robert's virtue and asking him to lead 'us' to heaven.

28. f. 60v.

'Soli Deo honor et gloria.'

29. ff. 60v–63r.

'De initio creacionis Ordinis Sancte Trinitatis.'
'Almyghty Lord in mageste . . . To myrth þat neuer mare sall haue end.'

Fifty-nine rhyming couplets in English describing the foundation of the Order of the Holy Trinity. This is printed below, pp. 72–76. Abb. *D*.

30. f. 63r–v.

'A prayer.'
'Hayle! cheftane, Cristes aghen confessour, . . . Ryghtwys Roberd, pray for þis! Amen.'

A prayer in eighteen English rhyming couplets for the house of which Robert is patron saint and for the speaker himself. He also asks Robert to help him at the last, that he may be saved from the fruits of his sin. This is printed below, pp. 76–77. Abb. *P*.

The manuscript measures approximately 8 by $5\frac{5}{8}$ in., and contains 64 leaves; it is of vellum with a nineteenth-century binding.

---
[1] See note to l. 1 for the emendation.

Introduction

The average number of lines to a page is 24, and the writing seldom goes beyond the limits imposed by four ruled red lines, two vertical and two horizontal. All the writing is in single columns except Nos. 1, 2, 4, 5, 7, 15, and 18 above, where the verse is written in stanza form in double columns, the last line of the stanza being written beside the penultimate. The other exception is the bottom of f. 15^v and the whole of f. 16^r, where the chapter headings for the following life of Robert are given in two columns. In the other pieces it is only an occasional section heading that is to be found at the side. The manuscript is written throughout in a single hand; it is usually quite legible, though occasional blots give difficulty. A few contractions are found.[1]

A rubricated heading occurs at the beginning of nearly every section, and the initial letters of these are also usually red, and sometimes decorated. In addition, a red letter occurs at the beginning of every stanza in the Latin verse, and of every couplet of the verse-pieces written in this form, except Nos. 26, 29, and 30. Red lines are used to enclose catchwords, &c., and occasionally for underlining. One marginal reference is in red, and initial letters in a line sometimes have a red stroke through them.

The margins of the manuscript have been defaced by words and scribble-marks in a later hand, and among the words which can be made out are the names of Thomas and Bryan Flemynge which occur several times. These may perhaps have been owners of the manuscript at some time, but they have not been identified.

There are two spare leaves of the same date as the binding at each end, and the fly-leaf at the beginning bears the following inscription in the hand of Henry Drury, who printed the texts given below for the Roxburghe Club in 1824.

In the top right-hand corner:

B^d by LEWIS. C. 7. 3.
H. Drury. Harrow

Then below that:

These are unique and unprinted Memorials of St. Robert of Knaresborough; and extremely curious—I printed one portion, the Metrical

---

[1] For details of contractions and of punctuation see Introduction, below, pp. 37–39.

Life, for the Roxburghe Club; and add beneath a note I received from F. Douce Esqr. who was kind enough to look through the Ms.

'Robert Flower the celebrated hermit of Knaresborough was according to tradition son of the Mayor of York. He lived in the reign of King John who visited him in his cell and bestowed upon him lands &c as mentioned in the present volume where a curious question that he asked the King is recorded.

This person is supposed to have founded the order of Robertines or Trinitarians; but its history is very obscure, as are the accounts of Robert himself who has been confounded with another person of that name mentioned by Matthew Paris as living near a century after the reign of King John and who is elsewhere made an Abbot of Knaresborough. The Cell in which Robert lived is still remaining at Knaresborough where they used to sell an abridged account of him originally compiled by Gent of York, under the title of "piety displayed", 12mo. The hermitage is also described by Leland in his Itinerary, I. 98.

Bishop Gibson seems to have been acquainted with some legendary account of Robert. See his Camden, under Knaresborough.

I have not yet discovered any other Ms. legend in old English verse but there is a life of St. Robert by one Stodley among the Harleian Mss. No. 3775.[1]

The present Ms. contains three lives of St. Robert, the first in Latin rhyming triplets,[2] the second in Latin prose;[3] the third in English verse.[4] All or some of these may have been compiled by some monk or hermit of Knaresborough perhaps by the president (as he here calls himself) of the order of Trinitarians who has a metrical prayer to St. Robert to aid him in the discharge of his official duties, &c.[5]

The rest of the Ms. consists of invocations in Latin and English to the Saint, and near the end is an account in English verse of the foundation of the order of the holy Trinity.[6]

Whoever was the author of the English life he seems to have had a better knack at this sort of composition than most or perhaps any of his contemporaries; and his lines are unusually smooth and harmonious. The description of the appearance to Robert of his mother's ghost is particularly deserving of notice. Her reappearance to thank him for the prayers he had successfully offered for her suffering soul and her last blessing on him, are eminently beautiful and impressive.'

Before the seventeenth century there is no definite information concerning the whereabouts of the manuscript, but during that century it was kept at Knaresborough, as Nicholas Roscarrock,

[1] Appendix B. [2] Introduction, p. 1, No. 1. [3] Ibid., p. 4, No. 12.
[4] Ibid., p. 6, No. 26. [5] Ibid., p. 5, No. 23. [6] Ibid., p. 6, No. 29.

Introduction

who gives a summary of Robert's life,[1] states that he gained his information from 'the very Legend or booke belonging to Knarsbrough, wher his life is written in verse and proase, in Latin and English'.[2] A little farther on he adds that he saw the manuscript 'by the favour of my Worshipfull friend Mr Francis Slingsby who dwelt not farr from Knarsbrough', but this does not make it clear if Slingsby himself owned it or not.

After this nothing is known of the history of the manuscript till it came into the possession of the Reverend Henry Drury of Harrow who bought it for half-a-crown in the Borough of Southwark; it was during his ownership that he printed it for the Roxburghe Club in 1824. At the sale of his library in 1827 it realized £33. 10s.,[3] and it passed, either directly or indirectly, into the library of the Dukes of Newcastle. It was there in 1863, for J. R. Walbran acknowledges that he gained his information concerning the life of St. Robert from a manuscript borrowed from the Duke of Newcastle,[4] and the work in which he used this, *Memorials of the Abbey of St. Mary of Fountains*, was published in 1863. The manuscript remained in this library until 1938, when it was bought for the British Museum at the sale of the Clumber Collection.

PROVENANCE OF THE TEXTS

There are two criteria which can be used to indicate in approximately which area the texts were composed—phonology and inflexional endings. Since the works are in verse it is possible to discover whether the rhyme-forms appearing in the manuscript were original or not.

A. *Phonology*

1. OE. $\bar{a}$ appears as a, ai, ay in rhymes with:

   i. OE. a, lengthened to $\bar{a}$ in open syllables of dissyllabic words.

---

[1] Camb. Univ. Lib. MS. Add. 3041, ff. 377^r–379^v.
[2] Ibid., f. 379^v.
[3] Details concerning the manuscript while in the possession of the Reverend Henry Drury are derived from W. T. Lowndes, *Bibliographer's Manual*, revised H. G. Bohn (London, 1890), iv. 2102.
[4] *Memorials of the Abbey of St. Mary of Fountains*, ed. J. R. Walbran (Surtees Society, 1863), p. 166 n.

ii. *ā* from Fr. sources.
e.g.
  i. *mare / care* M. 849-50   *care / rare* M. 607-8
    sare / bare M. 491-2   *haile / baile* M. 379-80
    wane / bane M. 325-6
  ii. *haste / Gaste* M. 45-46   *place / gayse* M. 575-6
    hame / blayme M. 957-8

ON. *á* is also found in a rhyme with ON. *a* in an open syllable in which *a* has presumably been lengthened: *wate / gate* M. 697-8. OE. *ā* remained as *ā* north of the Wharfe–Lune line, but south of that line OE. *ā* gave ME. *ǭ*. Three examples of such an *ǭ* are also to be found:

  i. Rhyming with OF. *ǭ* which has been lengthened from *o* before *r* plus a consonant.

  ii. Rhyming with OE. *o*, lengthened to *ǭ* in the open syllable of the stem of a disyllabic word.

Thus:
  i. *concord / lord* M. 481-2   *Lord / accorde* D. 1059-60
  ii. *euermore / before* D. 1013-14

The spelling *lord* is found in every occurrence of this word and in *lordyng* M. 370. Other forms with *o* from an OE. word with *ā*, not found in rhymes, are *so* M. 599, 618, 803, &c., *also* M. 467, D. 1070, *waloway* M. 552, 724, and *o* from ON. *á* appears in *or* M. 778, 842.

  2. OE. *ǣ*[1] appears as *e* in rhymes with:
    i. *ę̄* from OE. *ē*.
    ii. *ę̄* from ON. *é*.

Thus the nonWS. further raising of *ǣ*[1] to *ē* seems to have taken place. Examples of OE. *ǣ*[1] before dentals, &c., where *ę̄* could have been made tense, have not been used.

  i. *bere / here* M. 963-4   *wepe / slepe* M. 261-2, 317-18
  ii. *sere / brere* M. 435-6*

  3. OE. *ǣ*[2] has presumably become *ę̄* before *d* and *n*, and rhymes with *ę̄* from OE. *ē*.Nthn. shared this characteristic with a good part of the Midlands.

    weyne / cleyne M. 405-6   *wede / screde* M. 603-4
    dede / rede M. 923-4*

* This point should not be allowed too much importance, as perfect rhymes may not have been intended.

Introduction 11

4. OE. *ēog* seems to have combined to give an *ei* diphthong which has later been monophthongized, as regularly in the North,[1] to give $\bar{e}$, for it rhymes with OE. *ē*. The spelling *drye* may be metathetic.[2]

 dre / the M. 661–2   *drye / me O.* 1215–16

5. OE. *sc*, though written (*s*)*sh*, rhymes in a final unaccented position with (*s*)*s* from OE. (*s*)*s* or ME. *s*. This is a Nthn. characteristic.

e.g. *penyles / flesshe M.* 247–8   *this / fysshe M.* 285–6
  fysshe / iwysse M. 787–8   *was / asse P.* 1137–8

It is interesting to note in this connexion the rhyme *wyshe/blesse M.* 917–18. *ss* is the consonant sound that rhymes as both words come from OE. words with *ss*, but, because original *sc* is pronounced *s* and written (*s*)*sh*, here original *ss* is written *sh*.

6. OE. *æg* has been monophthongized and rhymes with OE. *ā*. This is again a Nthn. feature.[3]

 rayd / sayd M. 839–40, 853–4

(cf. the spellings *maden M.* 81, *fare M.* 490, where $a < æg$.)

7. Final *h* has been lost in *he M.* 409, 459, *O.* 1230, for the rhyme is with $\bar{e}$; this is a Nthn. characteristic.[4] Elsewhere, medially in a line, it is written *hegh(e)*.

Other phonological features may be mentioned, which, although they appear in the spelling, cannot be proved by the rhymes to have belonged to the dialect in which the works were composed.

8. OE. *e* appears as *y* after *g*; there has presumably been front diphthongization of $e > ie$, with later monophthongization. The only dialect in the nonWS. area which showed this change was Nh.: *forgyff M.* 455, 622, *gyff M.* 175, 596, 789, &c., *gyffen D.* 1020, *gytten M.* 830. A form with *e* does occur in *gett M.* 598, *O.* 1209, and this may be either from a form without diphthongization or from one influenced by ON. *geta*.

9. A. 2 above seems to suggest that OE. $\bar{æ}^1 > \bar{e}$, and it appears that this $\bar{e}$ has been shortened before two consonants, and that

---

[1] R. Jordan, *Handbuch der mittelenglischen Grammatik* (Heidelberg, 1934), § 101.
[2] Cf. Introduction, below, p. 38.   [3] Cf. Jordan, *ut sup.*, § 132.
[4] Ibid., § 198.

later the *er* has become *ar* in *farly M.* 328, *warlowes M.* 449, 709. This change originated in the North in the fourteenth century and did not spread southwards till the fifteenth century.[1]

10. OE. *y* appears as *i/y*, and in this feature Nthn. agrees with EM. Kentish influence need not be assumed for the few examples which show *e* from OE. *y*: *threst R.* 1294, *beried M.* 868, 872, 965; *e* may result rather from the influence of the *r*.

11. OE. *a/o* before a nasal generally appears as *a*, though *o* is found in *omonge M.* 85, *D.* 1045. Only WM. preserved *o* throughout.

12. The Angl. preterite *walde* is preserved as *wald M.* 33, 66, 258, &c.

B. *Inflexional endings and parts of speech*

1. (*y*)*s* is found in 3 sg. pr. indic.:

    case / hayse M. 657–8   *frendys / lendys M.* 129–30

No form ending in *eth* is found anywhere in the text. The *ys/es* ending spread from Nthn. to EM. *es* is found also in 2 sg. pr. indic., though not in a form with a rhyme, and this ending has also spread to 1 sg.:

    lyse / paradyse O. 1245–6

2. (*y*)*s* is found in 3 pl. pr. indic.; this is another Nthn. feature:

    has / place M. 989–90   *Saraʒyns / byndys D.* 1045–6

No form in *en* is found anywhere in the text.

3. The ending of the present participle rhymes with *and*. This spread to NM. from Nthn.:

    vndirstand / lyuande M. 49–50   *fand / dwelland M.* 139–40

4. The *n* of the infinitive ending has been lost:

    mette / swette O. 1247–8   *se / chastite D.* 1071–2
    vanite / be M. 43–44   *skath / bath R.* 1285–6
    begyne / synne P. 1141–2   *lede / red M.* 47–48

Nowhere in the text is there an example of an *en* ending.

5. The adverbial ending is *ly* and rhymes thus:

company / sekerly M. 497–8   *vnconnandly / forthi M.* 819–20
contynuely / mercy M. 921–2   *multyply / halely D.* 1111–12
ly / perpetuely M. 875–0   *prophecy / worschipfully M.* 845–6

[1] Cf. Jordan, *ut sup.*, § 67.

Introduction 13

Other points to be noted under this heading cannot be proved by rhymes.

6. The pl. imperative is found in *s* in *fles M*. 199, though *se* is also found, *M*. 121.

7. Where, in an OE. strong verb, the vowel of the pa. sg. differed from that of the pa. pl., the vowel of the sg. is found in the pl. of the ME. verb in the text: *bade M*. 234, *bare M*. 188, 940, *brak M*. 188, *raise M*. 233.

8. The only example of the pa. sub., *dang M*. 363, shows the same form as the pa. indic.

9. The *n* of the strong pa. p. is retained, unless, of course, the verb has gone over into the weak verbs: *seyn D*. 1082, *wretyn M*. 730, *D*. 1059, *gyffen D*. 1020, *gytten M*. 830, *tane R*. 1312, *gane M*. 830.

10. In most cases the weak nouns have taken the strong pl. ending *es/ys*, and only two, probably 'fossilized', *en* pl. endings remain: *oxen M*. 463 and *eghen M*. 362, 420. *en* plurals are rare in the North.

11. N. sg. of the third personal pronoun fem. is always *scho*, *sho*; this is again a Northerly characteristic.

12. The pl. of the third personal pronoun has *þ*-forms throughout. In dialects other than Nthn., *h*-forms, if not found consistently, at least vary with *þ*.

13. The Nthn. contracted form *bode* is found in *M*. 906.

There is a fair sprinkling of Old Norse words in the vocabulary,[1] but this feature, together with a certain number of characteristics listed above, is shared with the Midlands, particularly the East Midlands. There are, however, some specifically Northern or Northerly features—A. 1, 4, 5, 6, 7, 8, B. 2, 6, 7, 8, 9, 11, 12, 13 —whereas there is nothing that can be regarded as the exclusive characteristic of any other dialect.

Along with $\bar{\varrho}$ < OE. $\bar{a}$ (A. 1), which is definitely not a Nthn. characteristic, should be considered the rhyme *syght/heght M*. 593–4, where *heght* seems to be a Nthn. form introduced by the scribe which has spoilt the rhyme; for the rhyme to be perfect the sound should be non-Nthn. *i*.[2]

---

[1] Introduction, below, p. 15.
[2] NonWS. $\bar{e}$ (from the front mutation of $\bar{e}a$) + *h* has given $\bar{\imath}h$, either directly or through analogy with *hye*, but this $\bar{\imath}$ has been shortened before *ht*.

Although the majority of the examples have had to be taken from *M*., as the material available in the other pieces is limited, yet there is nothing in these that warrants the assumption that they were not composed in the same area as *M*. Since from the whole of *M*. only three examples could be cited of non-Nthn. rhymes, and only one from *D*., the next in length, it is not surprising that none is found in the rest, which are all much shorter.

From the evidence, the author of *M*. appears to have belonged to the Nthn. dialect area, but, since there are certain non-Nthn. characteristics, to a place not too far inside to prevent his using more Southern forms very occasionally, and in all probability the same may be said of the author or authors of *AME*.

DATE OF THE ORIGINAL VERSIONS OF ALL THE PIECES IN MIDDLE ENGLISH IN MS. EGERTON 3143

All the other pieces in Middle English (*AME*.) may be treated together with *M*. since they are closely connected in language and style.[1] As MS. Egerton 3143 is a collection of writings it would be improbable in any case that it contained the autograph copy of any of the works, and the improbable becomes the impossible when scribal corruptions are considered, e.g. *phannenne M*. 92, *heght M*. 594, where the rhyme is destroyed, and no doubt other instances, e.g. *hend M*. 395, *seryne O*. 1218, are also corruptions; they fail to make sense as they now stand. One cannot judge, however, how long a textual history *M*. and *AME*. may have had.

The dating can be only approximate as there is no internal evidence of much value. The upper limit is determined by palaeographical evidence and is to be put at late fifteenth century. The extreme lower limit should be the year of Yve's death, which is mentioned in *M*. 1007, but the date does not seem to be recorded. However, he was still alive in 1227, for it was in that year that the grant was made to him of land that Robert had owned,[2] and that year will then serve as the extreme lower limit.

It is possible to raise this by more than a hundred years since certain features in *M*. and *AME*. show them to be not unconnected with the poems of the 'Alliterative Revival' of the four-

[1] Introduction, pp. 9–14, 15–16, 24–25.
[2] *Charter Rolls, 12 Hen. III*, m. 10 (*1226–57*, p. 66).

Introduction 15

teenth century. Metrically the poems are to be connected with those which Oakden groups under the heading 'Rhyming Alliterative Works'.[1] Although these, unlike *M.* and *AME.*, are written in stanzaic form, yet the way in which they use alliteration and alliterative phrases—as ornaments rather than integral parts of the structure—and their composition in syllabic metres with end-rhyme, link *M.* and *AME.* to them.[2] In view of this affinity, *M.* and *AME.* cannot be earlier than the fourteenth century, and, since the alliteration appears to be used merely for the sake of ornament, the lower limit may be raised to the second half of the fourteenth century.

This would be in keeping with such linguistic evidence as the rhymes supply, though it is dangerous to attempt to date closely on these grounds. (Only the evidence supplied by the rhymes can be admitted, since forms found inside a line may be solely the product of the scribe.) The majority of the phonological changes found are such as had already taken place in the first half of the fourteenth century, but the diphthong *ai* is shown to have been monophthongized in the rhymes *rayd/sayd M.* 839–40, 853–4, and this development, according to Jordan (§ 132), did not take place until the second half of the fourteenth century.

In short, on internal and linguistic evidence, the composition of *M.* and *AME.* can be dated only approximately, i.e. between the second half of the fourteenth century and the second half of the fifteenth.

VOCABULARY

The vocabulary contains about fourteen hundred words, of which approximately 41 per cent. are French, 7 per cent. Old Norse, and 1 per cent. Latin.

Oakden[3] gives a list of the words not usually found outside alliterative poems, and some of these occur in *M.* and *AME.*: *carpyng M.* 38, *freke M.* 437, *lede* (people) *M.* 1, *reken M.* 687; verbs meaning 'to go': *kayred M.* 136, 207, 215, 959, *fared M.* 383,

---

[1] J. P. Oakden and E. R. Innes, *Alliterative Poetry in Middle English—Survey of the Traditions* (Manchester University Press, 1935), ii. 182 ff.
[2] See also Vocabulary, below.
[3] *ut sup.* ii. 175 ff.

437, 579, *found R.* 1270, *rayked M.* 583, 794, *weynd M.* 784, 837, *P.* 1162, &c.; 'stock adjectives of compliment': *fre D.* 1119, *O.* 1174, 1229, &c., *vn-frely M.* 194, *lele M.* 227, 527, *O.* 1204, &c.; 'poetical nouns': *wane M.* 829, and the 'specialised poetical sense of "person, child"' for *fode M.* 194.

Of the 'technical' words in the vocabulary the most interesting are those borrowed from the secular love-poetry and applied to the divine love: *paramoure M.* 4, *louer M.* 273, *luffly M.* 1.[1]

Finally, some of the words in the text are characteristically Northern or Northerly, such as *kytte M.* 163, *irke M.* 235, *hull M.* 409, *slyke M.* 44, &c., *teynde M.* 809, &c., *lathe M.* 646, &c., *kyrke M.* 236, &c. Several of these are to be found in rhymes.

Final *e*

Lack of stress caused the weakening and ultimate disappearance of most OE. inflexional endings, and in certain forms in the text final *e* may show a real stage in inflexional development, a stage current in actual speech at the time of writing, or one preserved in the writing from an earlier date. Forms of the infinitive show this. None preserves a full *en* ending, but some show apocope of the *n*, e.g. *haue M.* 512, *brynge R.* 1313, and others show the stem alone with no ending to indicate its function, e.g. *rest M.* 873, *weynd P.* 1162. Similarly the pa. pl. forms alternate between *e* and no ending, e.g. *come M.* 802, *herde M.* 927, *com M.* 186, *boght D.* 1118.

In other forms, however, there is no historical justification for the use of final *e*. In 1 and 3 sg. pa. of strong verbs in OE. there was no ending, though 2 sg. pa. had *e*. Forms in the text show an alternation in 3 sg. between *e* and lack of ending, e.g. *gaff D.* 1021, *gan M.* 173, *begane D.* 1080, *spake M.* 105, and one explanation for the appearance of such forms with *e* is analogy, perhaps from the 2 sg. pa. or from the pa. pl.

As far as the verbs are concerned it is not possible to work out any consistent principle which would govern the addition of unhistorical final *e* or the omission of historical final *e*; the only

---

[1] Also borrowed from the secular love-poetry is the 'May morning' convention, found in 297 ff., the setting for Robert's dream.

Introduction 17

process which will account for both is analogy. The same holds good for the nouns and adjectives. Just as in the pl. the nominative of masc. strong nouns (OE. *as*, ME. *es*) was adopted by other cases, genders, and classes, so it is equally probable that in both nouns and adjectives forms, which historically would have no ending, have affected those which historically would have *e* in ME., e.g. *son M*. 303 (OE. *sunu*), *well O*. 1215 (OE. *wela*), and vice versa, e.g. *duste P*. 1150 (OE. *dūst*), *hounde M*. 163 (OE. *hund*). Similarly *gode M*. 569 and *god M*. 997 (OE. *gōd*) are found; in both cases the adjective agrees with a noun in the accusative plural.

These last remarks may apply equally to the spoken and written languages, but a further point may be raised with reference to the written language in particular. If final *e* had ceased to be pronounced, either completely or in part, at the time the poems were written down, it would hold no meaning for the scribe, who would then tend to use it capriciously; there is no historical justification for pronominal forms such as *whame M*. 444, *paime D*. 1111, &c.

Another suggestion is that final *e* is used to indicate the length of the stem-vowel. It is not to be denied that this could account in part for final *e* as it is used in some cases, e.g. *wyffe M*. 392 (OE. *wīf*), *God O*. 1184 (OE. *god*), but there are sufficient examples to show that it is a principle that can by no means be applied throughout, e.g. *wyff M*. 81, *wytte M*. 765 (OE. *gewitt*). Perhaps in reality each of the points mentioned above has played some part in governing the use or non-use of final *e*.

THE ORDER OF THE HOLY TRINITY

The history of the Trinitarian Order in England has yet to be written. Deslandres' *L'ordre des trinitaires*[1] deals mainly with events in France, since it was in that country that the Order flourished particularly. It originated there and spread to Spain, Portugal, Italy, Austria, the Spanish Netherlands, and Great Britain. Beyond giving a list of the houses in England, Scotland, and Ireland, Deslandres makes but small mention of these

[1] P. Deslandres, *L'ordre des trinitaires pour le rachat des captifs* (Paris 1903), i and ii.

18 Introduction

countries because their role in the Order was of little significance.[1]

The *Catholic Encyclopaedia* describes the foundation of the Order thus: 'Its founder, St. John of Matha, a native of Provence and a doctor of the University of Paris, conceived the project under the inspiration of a pious solitary, St. Felix of Valois, in a hermitage called Cerfroid, which subsequently became the chief house of the Order. Innocent III, though little in favour of new orders, granted his approbation to this enterprise in a Bull of 17 December, 1198.'[2] These are probably the circumstances described with greater elaboration in *D.* 1083–1112.

The Order, thus established, was known as *Ordo Sanctae Trinitatis et de Redemptione Captivorum* since one of its main objects was to ransom captives taken during the Crusades. The habit of the brothers was white with a cross on the front, of which the upright was red and the cross-bar blue; one explanation of these colours is found in *D.* 1065–76.

The original *Rule* was not over-elaborate, but made the necessary provisions for the discipline of the Order in general and of the individual houses. Instructions were given concerning the regulation of the daily life, mentioning such points as clothes, food and drink, and works in which the brothers should be engaged. A complete list of the rules will be found in *Magnum Bullarium Romanum*,[3] and among the most important are the following:

The General Chapter, the governing body, originally met annually, but eventually the meeting was only triennial, and this naturally led to a decline in its power. Though the *Rule* affords little help, it is assumed that every Minister (i.e. every head of a house) had the right to attend.

At the head of the Order, elected for life by the General Chapter, was the Minister-General, with a Vicar-General as his deputy during absence or illness. From the end of the fifteenth century it was always the Minister of St. Mathurin's at Paris who was elected Minister-General. About the same period this house became

[1] Deslandres, *ut sup.*, p. 187. [2] *Catholic Encyclopaedia*, xv. 46.
[3] See the *Rule* given in a Bull of Innocent III, of 17 December 1198, in *Magnum Bullarium Romanum*, Laertii Cherubini (Rome, 1638), i. 52 ff., and *Mitigatio et declaratio Regulae* given in a Bull of Clement IV, of 7 December 1267, ibid., pp. 144 ff.

Introduction 19

the most important of the Order; it was already dedicated to St. Mathurin when it came into the hands of the Trinitarians, and, since the patronage was retained, this gave rise to another name by which the Trinitarians are sometimes known—the Mathurin friars.

The official next in importance to the Minister-General and his Vicar was the Provincial, in charge of a group of houses—in France twelve on an average.

Each house was to have a superior, usually referred to as the 'Minister' or 'Master', and six brothers, three priests and three lay brothers; later the number was arbitrary. One third of the revenue of each house was to be set aside for the redemption of captives, another was for the Minister and brothers, and the last third was for helping the poor.

According to Leland[1] and others, the Trinitarian Order was instituted in England by St. Robert of Knaresborough, who, they supposed, organized the community which lived with him. No evidence of such an establishment is preserved, but Leland may have been led to believe this because there was later a Trinitarian Priory at Knaresborough, which was known as the house of St. Robert instead of that of the Holy Trinity.

The date at which the Trinitarian Order was first established in England is obscure. The earliest date known for any foundation is that which Lt.-Col. Chettle gives for the house at Hounslow in Middlesex—'in or before 1200'.[2] Nine other houses in England followed this one, only two of them, Knaresborough and Walknoll, Newcastle, being in northern England. Papal Letters mention one in Ireland and four in Scotland. No reference to any separate Provincial for Scotland or Ireland has been found, and it is not unlikely that all the British houses were included in one province. One of the Provincials whose names are recorded, a certain William Puddesay, was Minister at Knaresborough before his election to the higher office, which he occupied for some years before and after 1400.[3]

[1] *The Itinerary of John Leland*, ed. L. Toulmin Smith (London, 1907), pts. i–iii. 86.
[2] H. F. Chettle, 'The Trinitarians and Easton Royal' (*The Wiltshire Magazine*, li. 365).
[3] *Papal Letters*, v. 551.

The Trinitarian House at Knaresborough

(For a fuller account of the history of the house see *V.C.H., Yorks.* iii. 296 ff.)

After the death of Robert on 24 September 1218,[1] Alexander Dorset, 'clerk', of Knaresborough, was granted the custody of the hermitage in 1219,[2] and in 1227 Yve, Robert's assistant and successor, was granted by Henry III the forty acres which King John had given to Robert,[3] and Yve, according to *D.* 1021–4, gave the hermitage to Coverham Abbey. Apparently the stipulation, made when the cell was handed over, was carried out for some time (*D.* 1025), but, for some reason unknown, the cell fell into disuse and was unoccupied until taken over by the Trinitarians.

On the same side of the river as St. Robert's Cave and the Chapel of the Holy Rood, but nearer Knaresborough, there are the remains of a religious house, which must have been that of the Trinitarians. As early as 1255 the Priory of the Trinitarians at Knaresborough was known as the house of St. Robert,[4] but no indication is given anywhere of the exact date at which the brothers settled there. Richard, Earl of Cornwall, issued a charter in 1257, granting the brothers the Chapel of St. Robert (thus it is obvious that it was not the site of the Trinitarian foundation as some have supposed)[5] and the lands which had been granted to Robert, along with additional privileges and grants of land.[6]

From this time onwards the history of the house is concerned with the granting of more land and privileges, both by the king and by important personages in the neighbourhood; of disputes on secular and religious matters; of additional building at the house, to further which indulgences were given to those who helped;[7] of the organization of the house and its numbers; and of the disasters which befell it through the depredations of the

---

[1] *Chron. Lan.*, p. 25.
[2] *Rot. Lit. Claus.* 3 *Hen. III*, m. 11 (i. 387b).
[3] *Charter Rolls, 12 Hen. III*, m. 10 (*1226–57*, p. 66).
[4] *Close Rolls, 36 Hen. III*, m. 5 (*1254–6*, p. 125).
[5] e.g. T. Tanner, *Notitia Monastica* (London, 1744), p. 681.
[6] W. Dugdale, *Monasticon Anglicanum*, ed. J. Caley, H. Ellis, B. Bandinel (London, 1812), viii. 1566.
[7] See e.g. *Papal Letters*, i. 277.

Introduction 21

Scots before 1318,[1] and the consequent relaxation of taxes to aid its recovery; until finally, on 30 December 1538, the Trinitarian house at Knaresborough was dissolved.[2]

ST. ROBERT'S CAVE AND THE CHAPEL OF THE HOLY ROOD

At Knaresborough itself there are two places connected with the name of St. Robert—St. Robert's Cave and St. Robert's Chapel—but there was only one place in Knaresborough where the saint actually lived,[3] namely the Chapel of St. Giles, and since we are told that the Chapel of the Holy Rood was built there also, this must be what is known as St. Robert's Cave, for the remains of a chapel are still to be seen there, bearing yet the name of the Chapel of the Holy Rood. Though often described as his home, the cave known as St. Robert's Chapel has no connexion with the saint.[4]

St. Robert's Cave is on the north bank of the Nidd near Grimbald Bridge on the Knaresborough–Wetherby road, and there the remains of a chapel, consisting almost solely of the ground-plan, are to be seen, with the cave itself in the cliff-side.

The west end of the chapel is on a different level from the east,[5] which has two steps up to the wall, presumably before the altar. In front of these lies the tomb of the saint (6 ft. 6 in. by 14–21 in.), with a hole in the bottom (15 in. by $6\frac{1}{2}$ in.). From the cave doorway round to the west end stretches a stone bench. An outer wall runs along part of the east and south sides and then joins the chapel wall.

At the foot of the steps from the road above, and more than halfway down the north side, is the entrance to the cave, which

[1] *Pat. Rolls, 12 Ed. II*, m. 26 (*1317–21*, p. 312).
[2] *V.C.H., Yorks.* iii. 300.
[3] See *M.* 386 where Robert returns to the Chapel of St. Giles *byfor whare he hade wouned a whyll*; this was in the Knaresborough district, and can only be, though the name was not mentioned earlier, the place where he lived first with the other hermit.
[4] Abbot Cummins makes this clear when he traces the history of the two oratories in 'Knaresborough Cave-Chapels' (*Yorkshire Archaeological Journal* [Leeds, 1926], xxviii. 80–88).
[5] 'East', 'west', &c., are used as technical terms since, strictly speaking, the east end is north-east.

22 *Introduction*

has three steps leading down into it. It is 17 ft. long and about 9 ft. 9 in. at its widest; the height varies between 5 ft. 10 in. and 6 ft. 3 in. Ledges and recesses have been hollowed out in two of the corners.

The cave has perhaps gained more fame as 'Eugene Aram's Cave' because of the tragedy enacted there.

THE AUTHOR OF *M*. AND THE RELATIONSHIP OF ALL THE MIDDLE ENGLISH WORKS IN MS. EGERTON 3143

In an attempt to establish the identity of the author of *M*., we must consider the possibility of his being also the author of one or more of the other Middle English works printed below, that is, of *D*., *O*., *P*., and *R*.

1. *Status of the authors of* M., O., P., *and* R.

The only direct evidence concerning the identity of the author of *M*. is found in *M*. 28–30, which proves only that he did not live in the house known by the name of St. Robert. *O*. is the prayer of the President of a religious house (*O*. 1181–3), who addresses Robert as *peirles patrone of þis place* (*O*. 1167). *P*. is again by the inmate of a house where Robert is considered as *pere and patron of this place* (*P*. 1132), but there is no indication that the speaker is any more than an ordinary brother. The author of *R*. tells us nothing about himself.

As far, then, as the status of the authors is concerned, there is no direct evidence to prove or disprove the common authorship of these four pieces. Therefore it is necessary to seek other evidence.

2. *Robert the patron saint*

By *Sayntt Robertys* (*M*. 30) it may be assumed that the Trinitarian house at Knaresborough is meant.[1] Again, since Robert is addressed as *patron* it would be naturally assumed that, in the other two passages quoted above, *this place* (*P*. 1132 and *O*. 1167) refers to the house at Knaresborough too. If this is so, then *M*. must be by an author different from the authors of *P*. and *O*., since *M*.'s author makes it clear that he was writing away from

[1] Cf. the note to l. 30.

Introduction

this house (*M*. 30), whereas *O*. and *P*. belong to the house of which he was patron saint, and there is no evidence to warrant the assumption that Robert was considered as patron saint at any other Trinitarian house in England.

3. *The connexion between* M. *and* D.

M. is complete in itself; it has its own prologue in which the author invokes Christ's help in writing his work, and nothing in it gives any indication that Robert has been mentioned before. It is, however, quite possible that the author of *M*. also wrote the description of the foundation of the Trinitarian Order (*D*.), for, if the prayer *Almyghty Lord . . . Grauntte me . . . þe grace þat I besoght before* (*D*. 1011-14) refers definitely to some previous supplication, then it may point back to the prologue of *M*., particularly 13-15, 32-34, where Christ is invoked; in the prayers *O*., *P*., and *R*. the invocation is to Robert.

The fact that *D*. begins at the point just after Robert is dead, whereas *M*. concludes after the death of Yve, with the result that some of the events of Yve's life are common to both poems, does not argue against the possibility of single authorship. On the contrary, *D*.'s author mentions the later events of Yve's life, and also the fate of Robert's cell until this came into the possession of the Trinitarians, in a way that suggests he was endeavouring to link the history of the saint and the history of the Trinitarians which he was about to write.

There is a point of similarity in the style of *M*. and *D*.; both pieces are written in an impersonal tone as though by an onlooker. We have already seen that the author of *M*. was not a brother at St. Robert's house; *D*., however, seems to go farther, giving the impression that the writer did not belong to the Trinitarian Order at all, as he speaks throughout of the brothers of that Order as 'they', and particularly is this seen in:

> Bott wyth all my hertt I pray
> To God þat he þaim saue & send.   *D*. 1126-7

Naturally, however, it would be much easier to believe that a Trinitarian was the author of a history of the foundation of his own Order, rather than that a non-Trinitarian wrote it. If a Trinitarian really composed *D*., he may have had a propagandist

24 *Introduction*

purpose in mind and so adopted an impersonal style to give his narrative an air of impartiality and historical truth.

Possibly *M.* and *D.* are by one and the same author, who belonged to a Trinitarian house, which was certainly not Knaresborough. As both pieces are written in a Northern dialect, it is not improbable that they were composed at Walknoll, Newcastle, the only other northern English house of the Order.[1]

4. *Verbal resemblances found in* M. *and the other Middle English works*

In the preceding discussion one possible link between two poems has been noted, *D.* 1011–14 *Almyghty Lord*, &c., which may point back to *M*. Two lines quoted above (*P.* 1132 and *O.* 1167) show a verbal resemblance, which is even more striking if the quotations are expanded thus:

Hayle! cheftane, Cristes aghen confessour,	
Als seruauntt of our Sauiour;	
Haile! Saintt Robert, thrugh Goddes grace	
Pere and patron of this place.	*P.* 1129–32
Hayle! Saint Robert, a confessoure	
þate suetely serued oure Sauioure;	
Hayle! peirles patrone of þis place.	*O.* 1165–7

Further examples of verbal resemblance between the five pieces may be advanced, but one example only is supplied for each link:

a. Yue ledde hys lyff lang in that sted	
Aftur the tyme Roberd was ded.	*M.* 1003–4
Eftyr the tyme Roberd was dede	
Yue wouned styll in þatt stede.	*D.* 1015–16
b. Than Robert, ay þat ryghtwys was.	*M.* 97
Haile! Robert, þat ay ryghtwyse was.	*P.* 1137

Cf. also *M.* 863 and 905, and *P.* 1164.

c. God for hys saike hys seruaundes saues,	
Nathyng denyes hym þat he craues.	*M.* 993–4
I beseke the, for hys sake	
Here þat nathinge the denied	
þat þoue aftur craued or cryed.	*R.* 1264–6

Examples, other than those quoted above or given in the foot-

[1] This house was dedicated to St. Michael (*Papal Letters*, xi. 586).

Introduction

note,[1] might be cited, but some of these involve the use of similar or identical alliterative expressions which were shared by many writers of this period. Indeed this usage may also explain some of the resemblances in passages cited in the footnote.

In one instance resemblance may be seen in subject-matter too, between the passage *D.* 1055–63, which expounds the meaning of the word *minister*, and the prayer of the President (*O.*), asking Robert to help him to carry out his duties as head of the house in the best way. With *D.* 1058 compare:

> And graunt me myght, strengh and grace,
> Þair simple prelate of this place.   *O.* 1235–6

and with *D.* 1060 compare:

> . . . this shepe
> Þat I haue cure of forto kepe.   *O.* 1227–8

The above-quoted examples of verbal reminiscences are surely not all fortuitous, even though rhymes and alliteration may account for some of the resemblances there found. Some stylistic connexion is thus suggested between all the pieces, *M.*, as the longest work, providing the strongest links.

5. *The relationship of the five pieces*

§ 4 points thus to a connexion between all five pieces. § 1 offers nothing definite to disprove a connexion between *M.*, *O.*, *P.*, and *R.* § 2 suggests that *M.* was composed in a different place from *O.* and *P.* § 3 points to a connexion between *M.* and *D.* and seems to agree with § 2. Apart from the verbal reminiscences, which may indicate some connexion between *M.* and *R.*, there is nothing to determine whether *R.* is related to the other four pieces.

The section on provenance[2] shows that there is no adequate reason to suppose that the pieces were not originally written in one and the same Northern dialect and about the same time. Such a connexion, which is strengthened by the evidence afforded

---

[1] Compare also *M.* 273–5 and *P.* 1137–8; *M.* 660–1 and *D.* 1047 and 1117; *M.* 337–8 and *D.* 1103–4; *M.* 993 and *D.* 1106–7 and *P.* 1136; *M.* 23 and 340 and *D.* 1061–3 and *P.* 1130 and *O.* 1166; *M.* 847 and *D.* 1057–8 and *O.* 1180–3; *M.* 847–8 and *O.* 1225; *M.* 242–4 and *O.* 1279–81; *M.* 689–90 and *R.* 1311–12.

[2] Introduction, above, pp. 9–14.

by the verbal resemblances (§ 4), must carry considerable weight in any argument in favour of unity of authorship; it would need strong evidence to the contrary, evidence which is not forthcoming, to make one discount the probability that the five pieces, if not showing unity of authorship, are at least the work of authors either living in or coming from the same area and belonging to the same literary school.

In view of the evidence, it is difficult to ascribe all five pieces to a single author. *M.* and *D.* may have had the same author, perhaps a brother at Walknoll; *O.* and *P.* were probably written at Knaresborough and may have had a common author, though there is nothing definite to suggest this; *R.* might have been composed at either place.

6. *The author of* M.

Two points should be noted about the hypothesis that the author of *M.* wrote at Walknoll.

a. His dialect was Northern, but occasional non-Northern forms are found which might suggest that he came originally from a place nearer than Walknoll to the southern border of the Northern dialect area. Perhaps he was originally a brother at Knaresborough who, for some reason, moved to the more northerly house. A fairly close connexion seems to have existed between the two houses, and the Minister of Knaresborough was charged with the visitation of Walknoll.[1]

b. There is a passage in *M.* which may lend support to the theory that the author lived at Walknoll:

        Than Robert . . .
        Purpost hym wyth page to passe
        Vnto this North Countre a-day,
        To Newmostres, the abbay gray.   *M.* 97–100

Robert is journeying north from York, and the impression is given that *this* is used because the author was living farther north than York and felt that the region to which Robert was going was in his own part of the North Country. Newminster is under twenty miles from Newcastle, so, if the author were at Walknoll, this

[1] R. Welford, *History of Newcastle and Gateshead* (London and Newcastle-on-Tyne, c. 1877), i. 158.

Introduction 27

phraseology would not be inappropriate. (Cf. also on this point the notes to *M.* 405 and *M.* 836.)

In conclusion, although there can be no positive proof, it is possible that the author of *M.* lived at Walknoll and was also the author of *D.*, but how far he may have been responsible for *O.*, *P.*, and *R.*, either in the actual composition or by influence, it is impossible to say.

THE RELATIONSHIP OF THE THREE LIVES OF
ST. ROBERT: *M.*, *EGERT.*, AND *HAR.*

The accounts of the life of St. Robert found in *M.* and *Egert.*, the latter in Latin prose, are complete and follow the course of his life from birth to death, but the life in *Har.*, in Latin prose, is defective. The extant parts of *Har.* correspond roughly to the first 400 lines of *M.* and the first eight sections of *Egert.* It is important that this deficiency be remembered, since any comparison between this life and the other two accounts must be limited accordingly.

The three works follow the same chronological sequence of events, *M.* and *Egert.* throughout, and *Har.* as far as it goes, apart from one incident which will be mentioned later. A careful comparative study of the works suggests a closer connexion between them than this surface resemblance, particularly between *M.* and *Egert.* The following four lists of similarities and dissimilarities between the three versions are based on a close comparison between *Har.* and the parts of *M.* and *Egert.* which correspond to it. The more important of them are discussed in full; references to the *Notes* are supplied for the rest where the significance may not be easy to estimate.

 A. *Har.* and *Egert.* in agreement against *M.*
 B. *M.* and *Har.* in agreement against *Egert.*
 C. *M.* and *Egert.* in agreement against *Har.*
 D. Important details found only in *Har.*

(A) Har. *and* Egert. *in agreement against* M.

 a. Fyff theffys com wyth mayn and myght.   *M.* 186
  Latrones ad eum divertentes . . .   *Egert.* 4
  . . . latrunculos . . . ad eius cellam veniendo . . .
              Har. 5 (p. 130)

Though the number of thieves is not mentioned here in *Egert.* and *Har.*, it occurs at a later point in *Egert.*—§ 14, but the part in *Har.* which would have corresponded to this is not extant.

>   *b.* Hys lyffe to lele men gaffe great lyght
>   Als doys a sterne apon a nyght.   *M.* 227–8

A similar passage does not occur at the corresponding point in *Egert.* or *Har.*, but one is found in *Egert.* 9; *Har.* is defective at the point corresponding to this.

>   *c.* Tway to the ploghe and ane to gay
>   Aboute the countre forto ta
>   Almos togedir in that land
>   For the poremen þat he fand;
>   The fourth seruaund, soth to say,
>   Hymselff to serue he held hym ay.   *M.* 267–72

In *M.* the duties of the third and fourth servants are the reverse of those in *Egert.* 6 and *Har.* 6.

>   *d.* Þe bred of this Goddes louer lele ...
>   In hys dysshe was na delytte.   *M.* 273–80

No similar passage occurs at the corresponding point in *Egert.* or *Har.*, but one is found earlier, in *Egert.* 5 and *Har.* 5 (p. 131).

>   *e.* Fisshe or flesshe whedir he toke
>   Fynd I nathing in my boke.   *M.* 281–2

Carnes quoque coctas sive assatas, gustato sapore, cito repellebat.
    Egert. 5

Carnes, gustatas nasi odore, omnino commedere respuebat.
    Egert. 14

Nullum denique edulium de creaturis quas anima movit sensitiva confectum voluit ore contingere.   *Har.* 5 (pp. 131–2)

This suggests that *M.* was not using *Egert.* or *Har.* as a source.[1]

>   *f.*   ... bott yff ȝe bowe
>   And dyng doune hys byggynges nowe,
>   I sall gar bryn yowe als a belle.   *M.* 347–9

It is Robert who is to be burnt if he refuses to leave his home in *Egert.* 8 and *Har.* 7, whereas in *M.* it is the servants if they disobey William's orders.

---

[1] But compare 'Troilus and Criseyde' (*The Works of Geoffrey Chaucer*, ed. F. N. Robinson [Boston, 1957, 2nd edition]), i. 132–3, where Chaucer denies having read whether or not Criseyde had any children. Boccaccio states definitely that she had none.

Introduction 29

(See also *Notes*, 143, 183–4, 213–14, 222, 283–4, 347, and 364.) The most important point of all these, one that cannot be explained away, unless it is assumed that the author of *M.* was concealing his knowledge for some reason, is *e*; this would prove that *M.* cannot be directly derived from either *Har.* or *Egert.*, since they both make a definite statement about Robert's not eating flesh, whereas *M.* maintains that nothing on this subject was mentioned in its source. The other divergences listed above, between *M.* on the one hand and *Har.* and *Egert.* on the other, suggest, not only that the author of *M.* was speaking the truth, but also that *M.* itself was not the direct ancestor of either *Egert.* or *Har.*

(B) M. *and* Har. *in agreement against* Egert.
    a. Thare bath they wouned in wyldernes
    And haunted full hegh halynesse.   *M.* 151–2
Habitaverunt itaque simul in loco horroris et vaste solitudinis ...
                                                                        Har. 4

There is no suggestion of such a passage in *Egert.* The fact that the second line quoted from *M.* does not find a parallel in *Har.* may detract from any value in the first line's resemblance.

    b. Þus the fend þes faytors fyff
    Fanded to fell hym fray hys lyff,
    Bott ay stalworthly he stode
    Agayn that foull vnfrely fode.   *M.* 191–4
... ille, cuius invidia mors introivit in orbem terrarum, ad infestandum Dei famulum sua excitavit membra, latrunculos ...
                                                                    Har. 5 (p. 130)

The *Har.* quotation occurs at a point slightly earlier in the story than that from which the *M.* quotation is taken, but nothing similar is found in *Egert.*

(See also *Notes*, 241–4, 251–5, and 342.)

The points in the above list are not as convincing as those in List A, but, if allowed, they may suggest that *M.* and *Har.* have some relationship independent of *Egert.*, and will confirm the evidence of List A which implies that *M.* is not directly derived from *Egert.*

(C.) M. *and* Egert. *in agreement against* Har.
    a. Bot þe fend, þat ys oure fell enmy ...
    Bott als a wreche wentt to hys wyffe.   *M.* 153–62

30 *Introduction*

... milite heremita, instigante diabolo, ... ad uxorem et filios reverso ... *Egert.* 3

The description of the devil's attack on the other hermit is much more elaborate in *M.* than in *Egert.*, but the devil is not mentioned at all in *Har.* as the reason for the hermit's departure. A better one is given there, namely that King Richard, whose persecution had led the knight to seek the disguise of a hermit, died, and so the knight was free to return home (*Har.* 4).

b.	Bott ay stalworthly he stode.	*M.* 193
	Non enim vir Dei propter hoc turbatur.	*Egert.* 4
	Conturbatum est igitur cor eius intra se.	*Har.* 5 (p. 130)

Here *Har.* is in opposition to the other two.

c.	And full playnly he enpeched Monkes vnmeke in þare presence.	*M.* 230–1
	Monachos de suis insolenciis palam arguebat.	*Egert.* 5

There is nothing in *Har.* that corresponds to this.

d.	On hym thei raise all in a routte And bade this blyssed mane gay oute.	*M.* 233–4
	Unde ab eisdem dissolute viventibus et sue sanctissime conversacioni invidentibus inpugnatus ...	*Egert.* 5

There is nothing in *Har.* that quite corresponds to this.

e.	Sothen wyth saltte and serued tytte.	*M.* 279
	... adiecto sale ...	*Egert.* 5
	... sine sale ...	*Har.* 5 (p. 131)

Har. contradicts the other two.

f.	A! myghty men, haue mynd of this ... Haue mynd of mesor, man and wyffe.	*M.* 285–93
	O vos delicati viri ... ante mentis occulos ponite.	*Egert.* 5

These two passages may not be completely parallel since *M.* does not here mention Robert's clothes, but there is no trace of any such apostrophe in *Har.*

(See also *Notes*, 185, 202–5, 262–4, and 337–40.)

Of the points enumerated in this list, the most important are *a*, where the divergence is obvious, and *b* and *e*, where *Har.* contradicts the other two. The instances in which *Har.* has no parallel at all—*c*, *d*, and *f*—may be in themselves small points, but it is

Introduction 31

not without significance that *Egert.* and *M.* do agree against *Har.* even in such details. Although *Egert.* and *Har.* agree against *M.* in some important points, yet the close resemblance between *Egert.* and *M.*, demonstrated above, is further illustrated by a comparison covering the whole of the two works; this reveals a strong resemblance, particularly in the manner of the narration of incidents. (See also *Notes*, 460.)

(D) *Important details found only in* Har.

The close agreement of *M.* and *Egert.* is further shown by the fact that in certain instances *Har.* supplies information, often of value, which is given neither in *M.* nor in *Egert.* The inclusion of moral passages may be ignored since these are no doubt to be attributed to the approach of the author to his subject. On two occasions additional incidents are mentioned:

a. After the attack made on his goods by thieves, Robert simply flees to Spofforth in *M.* and *Egert.*, but in *Har.* 5 (p. 130) he first returns to the matron with his tale of woe; she sympathizes and allows him to go to Spofforth, and continues to supply his needs.

b. When Robert decides to return to St. Hild's Chapel from Hedley, he asks the lady's permission (*Har.* 6), and she gives him more gifts than in *M.* and *Egert.*

Further details are added—the name of the widow who befriends Robert is given as *Helena* (*Har.* 5 [p. 130]); more information is given about St. Hild's Chapel which she grants him (ibid.); Robert's stay at Spofforth is said to have lasted six months (§ 5 [p. 130]); the connexion of the monks of Hedley with Holy Trinity Priory, York, is mentioned (§ 5 [p. 131]); and we are told that Robert went barefoot all his life (ibid.). It must also be noted that *Har.* makes no mention of the appearance to Robert of his mother (*M.* 297–326, *Egert.* 7). It is not impossible that this was in the lost part of the manuscript.

In view of the additional information supplied by *Har.*, it is hard to believe that *Har.* was the source of either *Egert.* or *M.*, for, if it had been, there is no good reason to show why they too did not include this information.

If we are to believe the author of *M.* in § A. *e* above, and if

List B is allowed, the conclusions to be drawn from the lists are:
- a. No one life is the immediate source of any of the others.
- b. *Egert.* and *M.* have a connexion independent of *Har.*, and similarly *Egert.* and *Har.* of *M.*, and *Har.* and *M.* of *Egert.*
- c. The closest relationship of any exists between *Egert.* and *M.* (Lists C and D).

On such evidence a table of affinity may be suggested:

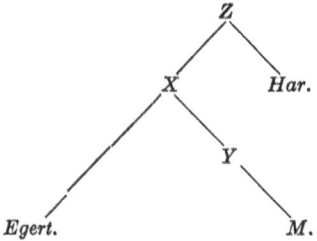

Z is the common source of all three and contains those points which they all share, and, in addition, it contains the points found in Lists A and B. *X* contains the features *Egert.* and *M.* have in common, including those they share against *Har.* (List C), and those found in Lists A and B. *Y* contains the points in Lists B and C.

The points in List C, found in *X* and *Y*, may have been derived from *Z*, and then presumably omitted in *Har.*, but they may be the product solely of the author of *X*.

If the author of *M.* suppressed his knowledge in § A. *e*, then *Y* may be omitted; the points in which *M.* differs from *Har.* and *Egert.* (List A) are then to be attributed to the author of *M.* himself in his use of *X*.

This is the basic form in which the relationship can be demonstrated, but it is by no means improbable that one or more versions came in between any of the two stages given here. There is no way of deciding whether *M.* was the first account written in the vernacular or whether, at some stage previous to *M.*, the Latin account had been translated into English or into Anglo-French.[1]

[1] See also note to l. 899.

Introduction

THE POSITION OF *LVL*. (*LATIN VERSE LIFE—EGERTON* 1) WITH REGARD TO *M*., *EGERT*., AND *HAR*.

(References to *LVL*. are to the numbers of the stanzas—see Appendix C.)

The Latin verse life of St. Robert, found in MS. Egerton 3143, comprises only 116 four-line stanzas. *M*., *Egert*., and *Har*. are similar in the amount of factual detail they contain in each section, though the two Latin lives indulge in much more moralizing than does *M*. If considered beside these three versions, *LVL*. appears a much abridged account, and consequently a comparison on general lines only can be attempted.

All the important incidents in the other three versions are to be found in some form in *LVL*., but the proportionate amount of space allotted to them does not correspond, e.g. *M*. (561-4) devotes four lines to Yve's journeying barefoot, when he left a blood-stained track, *Egert*. (§ 14) three lines, and *LVL*. (53) one stanza (*Har*. is defective at this point). In contrast *M*. (327-482) devotes 156 lines to the story of William de Stuteville's persecution of Robert, *Egert*. (§§ 8-10) 113 lines, but *LVL*. (31-42) only twelve stanzas.

Although the important incidents deal with the same subjects, there are instances where there is a change in the order of narration. Compare *LVL*. (13 ff.) with *M*. (89-184) and *Egert*. (§§ 1-3), where the incidents are reversed. Other incidents again have been cut down, e.g. only half the story of William's persecution of Robert is given, for whereas in *M*. and *Egert*. William intends to raze Robert's new home, but is prevented by a vision, in *LVL*. (31 ff.) the vision stops him from razing the first home. Though the account is incomplete, yet *Har*. (§ 7) shows that the same order as in *M*. and *Egert*. is being followed. In addition to the major changes, there are throughout small points of divergence; for instance, when William grants food to Robert's poor followers, to thirteen in *M*. 472 and *Egert*. 10, but to twelve in *LVL*. 41.

If allowance is made for the fact that *LVL*. is a much shorter work than *Egert*. and *M*., and that it might therefore be expected to omit much of the detail included in these, yet that does not explain the changes of order and other differences. It is not altogether improbable that there is some slight connexion between *LVL*. and the other three lives, since all the important incidents contained in *M*. and *Egert*.—and *Har*. as far as it goes—are to be found in it in some form. But if *LVL*. derives from one of the other works or their sources, then it is obvious that the author of *LVL*.—or one of his predecessors—has treated the account he found with great freedom, expanding, abridging, and altering just as it suited him best, so that in some respects it could be called an original composition.

CHRONICON DE LANERCOST (CHRON. LAN.)

The *Chronicon de Lanercost*, written in Latin prose, and from the Carlisle district, gives an abbreviated account of the life of St. Robert, dealing in any detail with only four incidents—the hermit who fled from Knaresborough, Robert and William de Stuteville, King John's visit to Robert, and the demand for tithes by the Rector of Knaresborough. Interesting details derived from this account are mentioned in the *Notes*, see 125–6, 161–2, 330, 463 ff., 737, 807 ff., 943.

A COMPARISON BETWEEN *HT*. (*EGERTON* 2) AND *D*.
(References to *HT*. are to the numbers of the stanzas—see Appendix D.)

D., in English verse, and *HT*., in Latin verse, describe the foundation of the Order of the Holy Trinity and show a correspondence in material, although this is not always presented in exactly the same order in both. In some places these two accounts run quite close together—*HT*. 11–14 and *D*. 1065–72; *HT*. 15 and *D*. 1035–7; *HT*. 28–30 and *D*. 1055–64; *HT*. 39–42 and *D*. 1113–24. In others the same theme is found in the corresponding passages, but the treatment is rather more individual; sometimes a fact found in one is omitted from the other. It must always be borne in mind that the Latin verse, with rhyme and alliteration in a shorter line than *D*., may account in part for some of the differences.

If we allow—what is quite probable—that the resemblance between the two is not fortuitous, the conclusion to be drawn is either that one is based directly or indirectly on the other, or

Introduction 35

that they had an ultimate common source. The statements made by the authors of the two works must not be taken too seriously, but the relationship that these would suggest is that *HT*. is based, directly or indirectly, on *D*., since the author of the former claims (*HT*. 31 and 36), and of the latter disclaims (*D*. 1081–2), a written source, at any rate for the description of the actual foundation.

THE REMAINING LATIN PIECES IN MS. EGERTON 3143

Since all the other pieces in MS. Egerton 3143 are closely connected with St. Robert, it is possible that some of them may have been composed by an author of a work in the manuscript which has already been discussed. Naturally, from their very subject, the Latin prayers asking Robert's help show some resemblance to the Middle English prayers, but the affinity should not be pressed. The references to specific occurrences in Robert's life are so brief that it would be idle to attempt to trace their origin.

This problem would seem to admit of little solution unless some significance, such as the possibility of common authorship or of close imitation, is allowed to the points of composition which some of the verse-pieces share. All of them show a fondness for rhyme, and, in most, alliteration to a greater or lesser degree is found in addition. Finally, *Egerton* 1 and 2 use the same metrical form, and *Egerton* 4, 7, 15, and 18 show variations on this. *Egerton* 10 and 11 share the same form, and in certain sections *Egerton* 3 follows this pattern too. The remaining five pieces are quite different or else contain only two or three lines. But, as it is difficult to estimate the importance of these resemblances, no definition of the possible connexion between the pieces should be attempted.

THE COMPILATION OF MATERIAL FOUND IN MS. EGERTON 3143

The question naturally arises, 'What was the object of the compilation of these prayers, &c., lives of St. Robert and accounts of the foundation of the Trinitarian Order?' An answer may perhaps be found in part in 'Officium de S. Ricardo de Hampole',[1]

[1] *The York Breviary*, ed. Lawley (Surtees Society, 1882), ii, Appendix iv.

which was prepared in anticipation of the canonization of Richard Rolle, a canonization which was never carried out.

The Office for Richard Rolle shows clearly in the rubrics the purpose for which it was composed; certain items in MS. Egerton 3143 are worthy of note as they seem to have been composed for a similar definite purpose. In 'Matutine de Sancto Roberto ex devocionem dicende' (*Egerton* 3), the prayers for each of the canonical hours follow the same pattern, four lines of verse, followed by a couplet, in some instances labelled 'antiphona', then a prose prayer, preceded by 'collecta', and a verse couplet. The next six pieces (*Egerton* 4-9) are likewise accompanied by some rubrics, but, though *Egerton* 10 and 11 may have found some place in an Office, yet there are no rubrics to indicate this, and the excessive alliteration and consequent straining of the sense suggest rather academic exercises.

The ultimate intention, at least with regard to its inclusion in this manuscript, may have been to use the Latin prose life of Robert (*Egert.*) for Lessons, just as the life of Richard was used, but the author's prologue gives no hint of any such purpose. The Life is divided into chapters with rubrics describing the contents, and each of these chapters could serve as a 'Lectio'.

The pieces *Egerton* 15-20 may be compared with 3-9 for they contain similar rubrics. Certain other prayers and apostrophes found throughout the manuscript—*Egerton* 13, 14, 21, 25, 27, and 28, some in prose and some in verse, and also the Latin verse life (*LVL.*)—may or may not have been intended for incorporation in a service; it is not easy to decide about them.

It is not improbable that the brothers of the House of St. Robert at Knaresborough considered that, because of the sanctity of Robert's life on earth and the miracles performed through him after death, he deserved to be canonized; and for this purpose they collected anything already written about him and composed other pieces, intending to send this collection to the appropriate authority to show that he was worthy of canonization. Perhaps *LVL.* 114 is a hint to this effect. Miracles performed by the saint after his death would strengthen the case, and such are mentioned particularly in 'Versus circa tumbam eius' (*Egerton* 22).

The brothers may also have hoped to use the material thus

Introduction 37

gathered together in an Office if the canonization were allowed, and MS. Egerton 3143 would then compare to some extent with *Legenda* prepared for Richard's Office, but as such a collection would be unlikely to contain all the pieces now found in the manuscript, the others—the English pieces and *HT.*, which has no obvious connexion with Robert—may not have been added till a later date.

But no record of the canonization of Robert is extant,[1] nor even, indeed, of any attempt to secure it, and there is so little to work on that any attempt to explain the compilation of MS. Egerton 3143 is unfortunately almost pure hypothesis.

THE TEXT

The text has been transcribed from rotographs supplied by the British Museum and collated with the manuscript itself. Modern punctuation and capitalization have been added. All the English writings in the manuscript are included, but the Latin prayer and ejaculations which are among them have been omitted. 'The Metrical Life of St. Robert of Knaresborough' (*M.*), the most important of the English works, is printed first, and is followed by 'De initio creacionis Ordinis Sancte Trinitatis' (*D.*)—1011-1128— and 'A prayer' (*P.*)—1129-64—which follow it in the manuscript. Then come 'Oracio Presidentis' (*O.*)—1165-1258—and 'Oracio ad beatum Robertum' (*R.*)—1259-1316—which precede it in the manuscript.

þ and *y* are written alike in the manuscript. At the beginning of the transcribed part there is often a mark above the *y* as if to distinguish it from the *þ*, but as such a mark sometimes occurs above the *þ*, no assistance is afforded. Difficulty has arisen in the transcription of the second personal pronouns singular and plural, particularly in 286 and 288 with the reflexive usage. No example is found elsewhere of the reflexive plural form, but the singular is *the* (e.g. 110), similar to the accusative and dative singular of the personal pronoun. Therefore the reflexive pronoun plural has been transcribed *youe*, which corresponds to the accusative and dative plural of the personal pronoun (e.g. 736, 432).

---

[1] See note to l. 17.

D

38 *Introduction*

ȝ is sometimes used to represent initial front *g*, but on two occasions it represents *z*: *Saraȝyns* 1045 and *cetiȝand* 1155.

i/y are used, as is to be expected, in the second element of diphthongs, but, in addition, they appear to be used to indicate a long vowel, e.g. *taile* 303, *keyn* 429. Final *e*, which, as mentioned earlier,[1] appears to have little significance as an inflexional ending, may perhaps be used to indicate length in some instances.[2]

A metathesis of *y* may account for one or two peculiar spellings in the manuscript. To give a perfect rhyme with *me* 1216 the vowel in *drye* should be $\bar{e}$; the original form may have been *drey* (*y* indicating length), and the scribe has metathesized in copying. Again, if such a metathesis had taken place in *key* 465, it would give an earlier form *kye*, which could easily be derived from OE. $c\bar{y}$. ON. *ei* and OF. *ai* might be expected to give *ay* in Middle English, and this is found in certain forms, e.g. *kayred* 136, *cayteyff* 607, but in others the metathesis is found, e.g. *caryed* 215, *catyeff* 400, *catyefte* 1296.

Apart from obviously essential expansions of manuscript abbreviations, e.g. p^9late to *prelate*, only such contractions as ‾ or ⌒ over *u*, *n*, or *m* have been expanded, i.e. to *un*, *nn*, and *mm*. Lines are often found, particularly through the loop of an *h* or a combination containing *h*, but since expansion seems unnecessary they have been ignored. Similarly a curled line at the end of a word may represent final *e*, but, as the use of uncontracted final *e* is so irregular, this curled line has also been ignored.

The expansion of the manuscript sign ꝭ, which represents a verbal ending or the ending of a noun in the plural, could be to *es* or *ys/is*. It has been expanded to *ys* on the following grounds, though it must be admitted that they may not really carry much weight. *ladys* 42 is the only instance in which *ys* is to be preferred from a phonological point of view, since OED. gives no example of the occurrence of the word without *i/y* representing final OE. *ig* except *lade* (*Sir Gawain and the Green Knight*, 1810),[3] although the forms *lauede* and *leuede* are cited in the 'Illustration of Forms'. The text is Northern, and *ys/is* forms are therefore not out of

---

[1] Introduction, above, pp. 16–17.   [2] Ibid., p. 17.
[3] *Sir Gawain and the Green Knight*, ed. J. R. R. Tolkien and E. V. Gordon (Oxford, 1936).

Introduction

place. Very few *ys* forms are found apart from the expansions, and it is possible that the scribe tended to render them by this contraction, a tendency produced by his rendering *is* thus in Latin texts, such as those found in the same manuscript, where ẜ never stands for *es*. Since *y* forms by far outnumber *i* forms in the spelling of this text, it therefore seems better to expand to *ys* rather than to *is*.

Perhaps *y* forms should also be used throughout for the expansion of the contraction ⁊, but in the case of *er/yr* (*ir*) in uncontracted forms there is fairly regular alternation and consequently each word has been considered separately.

Letters in round brackets in the text, and also in the Appendixes, indicate a conjectural reconstruction of a word where the manuscript is almost illegible. Omissions are rectified thus: *He⟨r⟩*.

SELECT BIBLIOGRAPHY

MANUSCRIPT

British Museum Manuscript, Egerton 3143, ff. 35ᵛ–38ᵛ, 39ᵛ–63ᵛ.

EDITION

The Metrical Life of St. Robert of Knaresborough ed. J. Haslewood (Roxburghe Club, 1824), presented by H. J. T. Drury.

HISTORY, CONTENTS, ETC., OF THE MANUSCRIPT

Cambridge University Manuscript, Add. 3041, ff. 377ʳ–379ᵛ.

Flower, Robin. 'Manuscripts from the Clumber Collection' (*British Museum Quarterly*, xii. 79–82).

Lowndes, W. T. *Bibliographer's Manual*, revised H. G. Bohn (London, 1890), iv. 2102.

LATIN VERSIONS OF THE LIFE OF ST. ROBERT

Chronicon de Lanercost, ed. J. Stevenson (Bannatyne Club, 1839), pp. 25–27.   abb. *Chron. Lan.*

Latin prose life of St. Robert found in British Museum Manuscript, Egerton 3143, ff. 15ʳ–31ᵛ.   abb. *Egert.*

Latin verse life of St. Robert found in British Museum Manuscript, Egerton 3143, ff. 1ʳ–7ᵛ.   abb. *LVL.*

Latin prose life of St. Robert found in British Museum Manuscript, Harley 3775, ff. 74ʳ–77ʳ.   abb. *Har.*

'Vitae S. Roberti Knaresburgensis', ed. P. Grosjean (*Analecta Bollandiana*, lvii. 364–400).

HISTORICAL BACKGROUND

Calendar of Charter Rolls.   abb. *Char. Rolls.*
Calendar of Close Rolls.   abb. *Close Rolls.*
Calendar of Papal Registers. Papal Letters.   abb. *Papal Letters.*
Calendar of Patent Rolls.   abb. *Patent Rolls.*
Catholic Encyclopaedia, xv.

Clay, Rotha M. *The Hermits and Anchorites of England* (London, 1914).

Deslandres, P. *L'ordre des trinitaires pour le rachat des captifs* (Paris, 1903), i and ii.

Dictionary of National Biography, xlviii.

Drake, F. *Eboracum: or the History and Antiquities of the City of York* (London, 1736).

Dugdale, W. *Monasticon Anglicanum*, ed. J. Caley, H. Ellis, B. Bandinel (London, 1812).

Excerpta e Rotulis Finium, ed. T. D. Hardy (Record Commission, 1835), i.   abb. *Rot. Fin.*

Select Bibliography

Farrer, W. *Early Yorkshire Charters* (Edinburgh, 1914), i.
Gent, T. 'Piety Display'd: in the Holy Life and Death of the antient and celebrated St. Robert, Hermit, at Knaresborough' (*Yorkshire Chapbooks, First Series*, ed. C. A. Federer [London, 1889], pp. 257–75).
Grainge, W. *The History and Topography of Harrogate, and the Forest of Knaresborough* (London, 1871).
Hargrove, E. *The History of the Castle, Town and Forest of Knaresbrough, with Harrogate* (Knaresborough, 1809).
Knowles, D. *The Religious Houses of Medieval England* (London, 1940).
Memorials of the Abbey of St. Mary of Fountains, ed. J. R. Walbran (Surtees Society, 1863), note on pp. 166–71.
Rotuli de Libertate ac de Misis et Praestitis, regnante Johanne, ed. T. D. Hardy (Record Commission, 1844). abb. *Rot. Lib.*
Rotuli Litterarum Clausarum, ed. T. D. Hardy (Record Commission, 1833 and 1844), i. and ii. abb. *Rot. Lit. Claus.*
Rotuli Litterarum Patentium, ed. T. D. Hardy (Record Commission, 1835), i, pt. i. abb. *Rot. Lit. Pat.*
Smith, L. Toulmin. *The Itinerary of John Leland* (London, 1907), pts. i–iii.
Solloway, J. *The Alien Benedictines of York* (Leeds, 1910).
Tanner, T. *Notitia Monastica* (London, 1744).
The Victoria History of the Counties of England, Yorkshire (London, 1913), iii. abb. *V.C.H., Yorks.*
Wheater, W. 'Vert and Venison' (*Old Yorkshire, Second Series* [Leeds, London, 1885]).

(References are made in the *Notes* to the works by Drake, Gent, Grainge, Hargrove, and Wheater, but they cannot be regarded as first-class authorities on the subject. The interest of these authors lies principally in a historical survey of the particular district or town with which they are respectively concerned, and the story of St. Robert is only incidental. For facts relating to Robert's life they are not reliable, dependent usually on legend, or the later writers in the group on the earlier, but with regard to names of places and suggested connexions with the story, their value is greater.)

f. 39ᵛ *De vita et conversacione Sancti Roberti iuxta Knaresburgum*

Prologus.

Thou luffly Lord of ylkay lede,
Crist, þat we knaw by our crede,
And God that ys our gouernoure,
That luffys all lele men paramoure,
And maker ys of all mankynd,   5
Thatt man has maste her in thi mynd,
Þatt sytt sall sothely by theselff
In sege to deme the tribes twelff
Of Yraell—als clerkys kan proffe
Þat forsakes all for thi loffe—   10
And called ys God of Abraham.
Our Lorde, þat lykkend ys to a lambe,
I beseke the, whare I sytte,
Visett þat thou wald my wytte
Wyth wysdom of thi worthi well   15
This lyffyng trewly forto tell
Of Saintt Robertt, þat heremytte
Was approued here perfytte,
Besyde Knaresburgh in a skerre
In a creues closed hym ferre,   20
And full deuoutely he lay
In contemplacion nyght and day

f. 40   In seruice of our Sauioure,
Als solitary dose day and houre;
And howe he lyffed in þat caue,   25
Efter the konnyng þat I haue,
Þat treuly whilk I to me toke,
Enformed als I was by a boke
That was sentt me by a frere
Fray Sayntt Robertys to me her;   30

12. Iohannes *in red in inner margin in hand of scribe*   17. heremytte *underdotted. Word erased in inner margin*   *Upper margin, f.* 40, *that in later hand*   29. a frere *underdotted.* a *and another word erased in outer margin*

Efter that boke sall I say,
Bott I purpose forto pray
To Cryst þat he wald sped my penne;
Þareto say ylk man 'Amen'.

De ortu & parentela Sancti Roberti.

Vhenn frendes fared well at a fest 35
And glewmen gladdes þaim wyth gest,
Of harpyng som has lyst to here
And som of carpyng of tales sere
Of Arthure, Ector, and Achilles—
Princes þat wer proude in prese— 40
Of kyngys and kempes, of conquerours,
Of lordys, of ladys, of paramours,
Þat ar bott vaine and vanite.
Of slyke sall noght my carpyng be,
Bott of a better he me haste, 45
f. 40ᵛ   Fadir and Son and Haly Gaste.
Somtyme in Yorke hys lyffe to lede
Off a ryghtwys man I red;
Toccus Flos I vndirstand
Men called hym when he was lyuande, 50
And his wyff Dame Suniuyte;
Sho bare a barne þat was perfyte.
Robertt I rede thei named hym ryght,
For bath he was stalworth and wyght,
Wyth thre faes to feght ay freshe, 55
The warlde, þe fend, and wyth hys flesshe;
Þir thre he felled wythowten fayll
And broght them down in playn batayll.
Than when this chyld myldest of mode
Couth spek and gang, he was full goode, 60
Of maners meke and of gud thewes,
Chaste and etchewand ay schrewes,
Deuoutt, deboner, and discrett:
A mylder man myght nay man mett.
Nouther he was wanton ne wyld, 65
Ne wyth nay foly wald he be fyld,

f. 41
    Bott dressed hym wyth deuocioune,
    Hauntand hympne and orysoune,
    Vsand abstinence ay fere,
    Fretand hys fleshe wyth fastyngys sere: 70
    That tyme nane toke hym wyth trispas;
    Off the Haly Gast fulfylled he was;
    In chyldhed chosen to chastite,
    Cheftane and chefe of charite,
    And of all vertues may diuerse   75
    Halff þan I may here reherce.
    In scoles, when he was sett to lere,
    He consaued mare in a ʒhere
    Þan hys felawes dyd in fyffe—
    Sway thoght Sayntt Roberte forto thryffe!—   80
    Wydow and wyff and maden myld,
    Þar company etchewed þis chyld,
    And yemed hys yeres well in hys youth
    By clargy als the chyld well couth;
    Omonge a thowsand an was he   85
    Þat was chosen to this degree;
    Ay wyth resone he rewled hym ryght.
    Cryst comforth hym ay als hys knyght!

f. 41ᵛ
    Quomodo Robertus factus est subdiaconus.

    Than Robertt, blissed in his brest,
    Purpost hym to be a prest,   90
    And to a byshope mayde hym boune
    And was subdiakenn wyth phannoune;
    And whi nay may orders he toke
    Fynd I noght brefed in my boke,
    Ne ʒytt the cause whi waytt I noght.   95
    He waytt þat waytt all þatt ys wroght!

75–76. *These two lines have been transposed*   75. a *in hand of scribe in outer margin*   *Cross in later hand in inner margin*   76. b *in hand of scribe in outer margin*   *Cross in later hand in inner margin*   90. Purpost: r *interlined*   92. phannoune: *MS*. phannenne   95–96. *Erasure of writing in later hand in inner margin*

St. Robert of Knaresborough

*Quomodo Robertus ivit ad Novum Monasterium
ad fratrem ibidem con⟨v⟩ersantem.*

Than Robert, ay þat ryghtwys was,
Purpost hym wyth page to passe
Vnto this North Countre a-day,
To Newmostres, the abbay gray,   100
Whare he hade a brother frere
Off letters lewed als som ys here.
When he was broght vnto his brother,
Swetly salussed ayther other.
Faythfully þan spake the frere   105
And sayd, 'Robertt, welcom here.
The rewle of this religioune
To proffe ytt wyth perfeccioune,
Wyth othir obseruaunce perfyte,
Dresse the, Robertt, wyth delyte,   110
By the counsayll of collacioune,
To com to contemplacioune.'
The presidentt þan of that place
Sway he gouerned hym by grace,
Hauntand hoge heghe halynesse,   115
Feruently fretand hys fleshe,
In praers bath and in pennaunce
Abydand, and in perseueraunce;
And off meruayles þat befell
May wyth mouth þan I kane tell.   120
'Se,' he sayd, 'all in this house,
Howe byrddys and bestys to Robert bouse;
Howe meke, how myld þat Robert ys!'
All meruailed off hys modynesse.
Foure monethes and tway wekys mare   125
Robertt reued wyth monkys þare.

Quo⟨modo Robertus⟩ reversus ⟨est Ebo⟩racum.

And than þis man, myldest of mode,
To Yorke agayn full myldly yode,

---

114. gouerned: *MS.* goruerned   125–31. *Erasure of writing in later
hand in outer margin   Above* 127. *Since the letters printed in brackets are*

46 St. Robert of Knaresborough

  To hys frenshipe and hys frendys,
  Bott lytell while wyth thaym he lendys.   130
  Wyth the Haly Gast this man inspired
f. 42ᵛ Nathyng bott God in erth desyred.
  Wythowten counsayll of his kynne,

  Quomodo Knaresburgum venit.

  Vnwettand all bath mare and mynne
  Bott God, þatt wyssed hym by and thrugh,   135
  He kayred and com to Knaresburgh;
  All thynge forsakand þat he sawe,
  Nathyng hym lyked bott Goddys lawe.
  Thar ane hermett Robertt fand
  Deuoutly in a roch dwelland,   140
  Þat a knyght had beyn befor,
  That tow(r)e and towne and hys tresour,
  All had forsaken, chyld and wyffe,
  And þare als hermett led hys lyffe.
  When this hermett Robertt sawe,   145
  'Welcom,' he sayd, 'my fair felawe!'
  And soyne he sayd wyth gud ententt,
  'Blyssed be God, þat me has sentt
  Swylk a felaw wyth me to woune,
  Þat dubbed ys wyth deuocioune.'   150
  Thare bath they wouned in wyldernes
  And haunted full hegh halynesse.

  Quomodo herimita in temptacione decidit.

  Bot þe fend, þat ys oure fell enmy,
  To þir tway had great invy;
f. 43 Bott Robertt myght he noght arest   155
  For nay fandyng maste ne lest;

illegible in the manuscript, they are conjecturally reconstructed from the sense of the following passage
 138. goddys *underdotted.* ..g.s *erased in inner margin* 140. Cross *in later hand in outer margin* 148. *The last two letters of* sentt *are not perfectly clear but can be made out.* 149. woune *is not very clear, but can be made out* *Above* 153. herimita: *MS.* herinita *Catchwords* Bott Robert myght *at right-hand side of lower margin, f.* 42

St. Robert of Knaresborough

To hys felagh forthi he ferd
And sway mased mayd hym and merred
That Robertt, wyth nay resone ryght,
Fray hys mynd amend hym myght. 160
Langir lyked hym noght that lyffe,
Bott als a wreche wentt to hys wyffe,
Als a hounde þat kastes out of hys kytte
And ay turnes and takys eft hys vomytte;
And forthermare kan I noght tell 165
By this fayland what befell.
Þan Robertt ranne hys saule to saue
And in a roche closed him in caue;
Off mannes solace nane he hadde
Bott grace of God þat mayd hym glad; 170
Wyth ympnes þis hermett þat was tryed
Gastly God he gloryfyed.

Quomodo ad capellam Sancte Hilde devenit.

Tyll on a tyme Robertt gan hy
Vnto a wydow þat wouned þareby.
'Dam', he sayd, 'to gyff me this day 175
Off thi almose I the pray.'
Than sayd þat wyff, mody and myld,
'Þe chapell I graunte þe of Sayntt Hylde,
Wyth all the land þat lyes partyll
Þat the lykys—this ys my wyll— 180
To the and thi poremene all ay;
Agayn my gyft sall nay man say.'
Þar Robertt wouned þan all a ȝhere
Wyth hys poralles in prayer.

Quomodo latrones eum spoliaverunt.

Tyll ytt befell apon a nyght 185
Fyff theffys com wyth mayn and myght;

168. *Cross in later hand in outer margin*   171. ympnes: *MS.* ympies
173–5. *Erasure of writing in later hand in outer margin*   184.
poralles *underdotted*   *Above* 185. spoliaverunt: *MS.* spoliaverit

Robertt to robbe þay ranne a-day.
Hys bour thei brak and bare away
Hys bred, hys chese, hys sustinaunce,
And hys pormen purueaunce.   190
Þus the fend þes faytors fyff
Fanded to fell hym fray hys lyff,
Bott ay stalworthly he stode
Agayn that foull vnfrely fode,
Hauand in hys mynd always   195
How God in hys gospell says,
'Yff foles pursue ȝow, fals and fell,
f. 44   In a cytee whare ȝe dwell,
Fles into another thanne.'
Þarfor Robertt rayse and ranne   200

Quomodo ivit Spoford.

And sped hym vnto Spofford towne
To serue God wyth deuocioune;
Þare he haunted halynesse
And affliccions of hys flesshe,
Vsand abstenence swa great   205
All men had meruayll of hys mette.
They caryed fra countres to hym þanne
To honore hym als ay haly mane;
Þai rosed hym doand reuerence
And peirles praysed hym i presence.   210
Bott when that Robertt vndyrstode
Vaynglory þat ay es noght gode,
He purpost priuely forto passe
Away whar þat hys wounyng was,

Quomodo venit Hedlay.

And caryed and come to ane abbay   215
Off monkes þat men calles Hedlay;
And thei resaued Sayntt Robertt fair
Yff he had beyn a myghty mare,

---

189. *In* sustinaunce *a blot covers the letter that must be* i *because of the stroke above it*   201. And: MS. Aand   *Above* 215. Hedlay: d *has been superimposed on another letter, probably* l *written first by mistake*

And benyngly broght hym in
Omang þase monkes mare & mynne.   220
All approued hym als perfytte
And cled hym in a coule of whytt.
Nathyng vndyrneth he hade;
Bott a coule—and þat was bade—
Mair to couerynge of hys skynne   225
Than for cald away to wynne.
Hys lyffe to lele men gaffe great lyght
Als doys a sterne apon a nyght.
Off perfeccioune oft he preched
And full playnly he enpeched   230
Monkes vnmeke in þare presence
Þat sett them vnto insolence.
On hym thei raise all in a routte
And bade this blyssed mane gay oute;
Att hym þay wex bath wrath & irke   235
Bath in closter and in kyrke,
And sway dered hym wyth þair dynne
Off messy þatt he myght noght mynne.

Quomodo revenit ad capellam beate Hilde virginis.

Than Robertt rewed and sair repentt
And to Saynt Hylde chapell he wentt,   240
Wele leuer to dwell wyth theffys mekyll
Þan wyth felaghes fals and fekyll,
Better to beld wyth bestys wyld
Þan wyth merred men and vnmyld.
When he was commen to hys chapell   245
In depe deuocions forto dwell,
Poremen that war penyles
He fand tham fode of fysshe and flesshe.
Iwys this wydow was full fayne
When sho wyste he com agayne;   250
Men off crafte swyth gartt scho call
To bygge Saynttt Robertt a honest hall,
And mansiounes for hys men gart make
And a lath for Robertt saike,

        Hys corne, hys catell in to brynge. 255
        Bott he etchewed ouer all thynge
        Wordes to speke of vanite
        Wyth freinde or fay; ay wald he fle.
        Ay to hys mette when he suld flytte,
        In sylence sadly wald he sytte; 260
        Hys visage waned swa wald he wepe,
        Opon a pamentt ly and slepe
        A lytyll space that dremyng droghe—
        Off slepe had he noght halff enoghe!
        He hired and had þaime to hys handes, 265
        Als scriptur says, four seruandes,
f. 45ᵛ   Tway to the ploghe and ane to gay
        Aboute the countre forto ta
        Almos togedir in that land
        For the poremen þat he fand; 270
        The fourth seruaund, soth to say,
        Hymselff to serue he held hym ay.
        Þe bred of this Goddes louer lele
        Þe fourth partte was of barly mele,
        Þe fyfht of as, wyth mesor maste 275
        Wele proporciond in a past;
        Hys potage was of cale and leke,
        Off other herbes þat he gartt seke,
        Sothen wyth saltte and serued tytte:
        In hys dysshe was na delytte. 280
        Fisshe or flesshe whedir he toke
        Fynd I nathing in my boke,
        Bott watir drang or ayll thynne,
        And ȝytt mesor was þareinne.
        A! myghty men, haue mynd of this, 285
        Þat fedes youe bath of flesshe and fysshe
        And all dayntes þat are dere
        And delytes youe in þaim here:
        When thou ys sett & semly serued
f. 46   And thi bred wyth knyffe ys kerued, 290
        Partte a porciounc vnto the pore:

    274–8. Ry.h . . . . . *in later hand vertically in inner margin*

St. Robert of Knaresborough

Sway dyd Sayntt Robert att hys dore.
Haue mynd of mesor, man and wyffe,
How Sayntt Robertt rewled hys lyffe;
To begge an brynge pore men of baile,   295
Þis was hys purpose principale.

Quomodo mater eius nuper defuncta eidem apparuit.

A tyme als Saint Robertt lay
In a medow, tyme of May,
In flouers slepand in a sted,
Appered hys moder þatt was ded,   300
Paile and wan of hyde and hew,
Roberd praers to pursue.
'Son,' sho sayd, 'tentt to my taile.
To blysse þou may bryng me fra baile
Thrugh help of thi halynesse.   305
Haue mynd I sufferd the of my flesshe.'
Roberd remed and rewed sair
And fraynd his moder of hyr far.
'Son,' scho sayd, 'yt ys noght to layn:
I am pressed and put to payn   310
For mettes and mesores maid vnlele,
For okir and vthir fautes fele;
For þir and vthir nyght and day
I beseke the for me pray.'
Þan Roberd raise and redy was   315
Vnto hys praers forto passe;
He syghed, he sobbed, he lytyll sleped,
Hys handys he wrang, and wyghtly weped;
To God he praed wyth Peter & Paule
Forto saue hys moder saule.   320

f. 46ᵛ

297. als *underlined*; as *in later hand in outer margin*   299. sted *underlined*; place *in later hand in outer margin*   303. tentt *underlined*; take hede *in later hand in outer margin*   304. baile *underlined*; sorrowe *in later hand in outer margin*   307. remed, rewed *underlined*; sighed & so.ed *in later hand in outer margin*   308. demamded *in later hand in outer margin*   311. mettes, mesores, vnlele *underlined*; mesores, so . . . . . *in later hand in outer margin*

Þan in the endynge of þat ȝere
Appered hys moder to hym here
And blyssed hyr barne þat maid hir blyth,
Sayand, 'My sone, now sall I swyth
Wend to welth þat neuer sall wane.   325
Farwele! I blysse the, blode and bane.'

Quomodo Willelmus de Stutivilla precepit prosterni habitacula.

Apon a tyme, als telles a texte,
Bifell this farly althir nexte.
Þare wouned a worthly lord a whyle—
Men called hyme William Scutivyle—   330
Lord of that land, bath est & weste,
Off fryth, of feild, and of forest.
Als this William wentt a-day
Byside Sainte Roberde place to play,

f. 47 He spirred and spared noght in that place   335
Whay bygged, wha belded in that space.
All thei answerd hym full tytt,
'Ane hermet, þat ys full perfytt;
Roberd, þat ys nay rebelloure,
A seruand of our Sauioure.'   340
Þan Wylliam fast began to flytte
And sayd, 'This ys ane ypocrytte,
Fautour, felaghe, and a fere;
Off all the theffys þat wounes here
A receptour Robertt ys,   345
And of my wyld all þat here ys.
By the eghe of God, bott yff ȝe bowe
And dyng doune hys byggynges nowe,
I sall gar bryn yowe als a belle:
He⟨r⟩ sall he nay langar dwell!'   350
Bott ȝytt hys seruandys dyd nay skathe,
Ne bowede noght to hys byddynges brathe,
Bott lett hys byggynges blythly stand;
Þai wyst þat he was wele lyuand.

St. Robert of Knaresborough

Quomodo prostrata sunt edificia eius.

    Bott sone aftyr þis befell   355
Þat this Wylliam I of tell
Wyth hys hondes hyed hym to hontt
Besyd the place whare Roberd wontt,
And sawe hys byggynges haile abyde.

f. 47ᵛ   He chawfed hym and byganne to chyde;   360
He banned and bost þaim forto bete,
And sware by Goddes eghen in hys threte
Bott yff þai dang hys byggynges doune
Þat he sulde gar crake þair croune.
Þan þai durst na langar byde,   365
Bott vnto Roberd housynge hyed
And dang them doune, bath lesse & mare;
Nathyng left þai standand þair.
Þan Robertt sawe and sayd þaim tyll,
'Whedir your lordyng wyll or nyll,   370
Besyd his tour and hys castell
Wythouten end here sall I dwell.'
Þis dyd the deuill—þis ys nay dowte—
Stirred þis steren man & þis stoute
Agayns þis blyssed man in bataill,   375
Wyth fandynge forto gare hym faile;
Bott ay stalworthly he stode
Augayns the fend; noght chaunged hys mode.
He sayd, 'My Lord, my helpe, ys haile;

Quomodo venit ad capellam Sancti Egidii.
Off man I dred nay bytter baile.'   380
When Robert saw all dongen doune,
Wyth his boke he mayd hym boune

f. 48   And fared all that forest thrughe
And come agayn to Knaresburghe,
To a chapell of Sayntt Gyle,   385
Byfor whare he hade wouned a whyll,

363–4. R R *in later hand vertically in inner margin*   367. Bo.t
.nomor *in later hand upside down in inner margin*   371–4. R . . *in
later hand vertically in inner margin*

54   St. Robert of Knaresborough

Þat bygged was in tha buskes wythin,
A lytell holett; he hyed hym in
And þare wyth depe deuocioune
He crepe in contemplacioune,   390
And als ane aungell lede hys lyffe,
Sway heghe, sway haly, þat man and wyffe,
Heghe and lawe, vnto hym hyed
In faith forto be edified.

Quomodo quis audivit vocem demonis clamantis.
A tyme was herd her of a hend   395
A voyce þus cryand of a fend,
'Allas! allas! I am the vyce
Þat kest outt Adam of paradyse,
And ȝytt I may noght wyth forfett
Ouercome þis catyeff Robynett;   400
Ȝit am I prest hym to pursue.
Hys noy sall now be euer newe!'

*Quomodo dictus Willelmus vidit vaporem fumi
ascende⟨n⟩tem.*

Eftirward a lytell while
The forsayd William Scutivyle
Outt of the North Countre, I weyne,   405
Come to Knaresburghe castell cleyne.
f. 48ᵛ   Bott als þis ryall was rydand
Wyth hond and hauke opon hys hand,
Out off Roberd hull full he
Rayse a reike þat men myght se.   410
Þan sayd Sir William merueland,
'What bemeynes ȝond reke rysand?'
'Sir,' ane sayd, 'out of a cote
Whare Robertt dwelles, a mane deuoute.'

388. *Cross in later hand in outer margin*   *Above* 395. Quomodo: *MS.*
Quodomodo   *Above* 403. vaporem: *MS.* vapare   *Upper margin,*
f. 48ᵛ, Robert.   John   And And And *in later hand*   409.
Cross in later hand in outer margin   409–10. Rob . . . *in later hand in*
inner margin

'What!' sayd Wylliam, 'ys þis he 415
Fray my forest þat I gartt fle?'
'Yha,' þai sayd, 'þis ys the same;
Off your wyld beres he na blaym.'
Þan Wylliam wex wytles and wode
And swar by Goddes eghen þar he stod 420
That he suld noght to bed be boune
To hys cotage ware casten doune;
Bott ʒytt þis Wylliam was of wyne
Sway dronken þar, als I deuyne,
Þat he myght noght hald hys athe, 425
Botte he sware he suld hym skathe
And doune gar dyng hys domicelle
Opon the morn, euerylkay dele.
Þus þis keyn knyght hym vncled
And busked and bouned hym to hys bed. 430

f. 49 *Quomodo tres ... erunt Willelm⟨o⟩ in grabato*

Bott off a ferly þat eftir fell,
Yff ʒe wyll lythe, I wyll youe tell.
Als William lay, moysand in mynd,
Appered thre men blakker þan ynd.
Tway droghe a trayle wyth pykes sere— 435
Was neuer sharper thorne ne brere;
Thyrd fared befor, a foule freke,
Wyth tway maces, þus to speke:
'Ryse vp, Wylliam, stythely stand,
And taik þis mace here in thi hand 440
And defend the wyth thi myght,
For fersly sall I wyth the fyght
For Robertt saike, þat nay man noyes,
Whame þou derfely doune distroes.'
Þan Wylliam, rysand of hys bede, 445
Bath hys armes full wyd he spred,
And 'Mercy' cryed full carefully
And sayd, 'My mysded mend wyll I.'
Þan þir thre warlowes vanist all away;
Wylliam sleped to ytt was day. 450

On the morne he raise out of hys bed
And full hastely hym sped

f. 49ᵛ *Hic precatur Willelmus veniam a Roberto.*

To Robertt holett, whare þat he
Befor hys fett fell on hys kne
And sayd, 'Roberd, forgyff me all 455
My greuouse gyltes; amend I sall.'
Roberd forgaff, and William kyssed
And blythely wyth hys hand hym blyssed.
Þan William sayd, 'Fray the roches he

Hic dedit Roberto possessionem & elimosinam.

To Grymbalde Kyrkstane gyff I the; 460
Land and lythe, all þat þare lyse,
To tyll ytt on thi best wyse.
Tway hors, tway oxen I the gyffe,
Helpe and hald here whyls I lyffe;
Tway key I graunte the of my grace 465
To all thi poremen of thi place;
Also sustinaunce I sall the send,
Fray Yole Day ylka ȝere to thend
Off dayes thretten folowand,
Tym þat I lyff in this land, 470
Almos bathe of flesshe and fysshe
For thretten men; sall they nott mysse.'
Þus messy, mast þat ys of myght,
Bath chastes conqueroure and knyght.
He kemmes the crowell wyth hys cambe, 475
Off a lyon makys a lambe.
He mayd hym meke þat Roberd merred
And mayd hym wardan in this werld;
f. 50 Hys sainttys in sorowe noght forsakes
Bott, them to comforthe, trewly takes 480
Wyrshype and wysdom wyth concord
And loueyng ay to be slyk a lord.

453. *Cross in later hand in outer margin*   459. *Cross in later hand in outer margin*

St. Robert of Knaresborough

Walterus frater eius & maior civitatis Eboracensis edificavit igitur domicilia cum capella.

This bifell þat I sall say;
Eftirward opon a day
Walter, þat was hys brothir dere   485
And Mare of Yorke full many ȝhere,
Com to Knaresburgh, als I rede,
Robertt to vysett in hys dede.
When he was broght vnto hys brother
Full fare salussed ayther other.   490
'Brother,' he sayd, 'me rewes sare
Þat thou beldes in thes buskes bare,
And specially in this spelunke
In wyldernes als dyd a monke.
Yff thou wyll leue and wend wyth me,   495
Whare þat þi liste ys best to be,
In couent, closter or company
I sall gar sett the sekerly.'
Roberd sayd, 'Nay! soth I the tell,

Hec requies & cetera.

Wythouten end here wyll I dwell;   500
Here haue I chosen ay forto won.
Farwell! in my benyson!'
When Walter wyst away he wentt;
f. 50ᵛ   He thanked God for hys trewe ententt.
Þan Walter wentt and sentt hym to serse   505
Werkmen wyse of craftes diuerse,
Hym to byge a chapell gode
In the honore of the Haly Rode.
Þare Robertt ryst hym, als I rede,
Irke ne ydell neuer of dede.   510

Quomodo Yvonem sibi sociavit.

Roberd vmbythoght hym þane
Wyth hym to won to haue som man

493. *Cross in later hand in outer margin*

To beilde hym wyth hys besines
þat he myght haunte hys halynes.
Furth he wentt ánd ane he fand, 515
Yue that men called in that land.
'Yue,' he sayd, 'comme, folowe me;
Off Gode a seruand sall þou be.'
Thus answerd Yue and to hym sayd,
'Off this tydynges am I payd. 520
I wyll forsake all þatt I se,
Fadyr and freynd, and folowe the,
Gold and good, ryches and rentt,
Towne and toure and tenementt,
Playng and prosperyte, 525
In pouerte forto won wyth the.'
Yue to Roberd ay was lele,
Hys almos helpe hym forto dele.

f. 51 To all þat pore was in þat place
Full trewly toke Robertt trace. 530

De temptacionibus Yvonis.

Sathan, þat sotell ys and quayntte,
Thoght to take Yue wyth a taynte.
He stirred hym stryffe on ylkay syde
þat Yue thoght bytter to abyde,
Bott Roberd wyth hys resons swett 535
Redy was ay hys bales to bett;
Bott ȝytte the fend forged hym a whyle
This blissed mane forto begyle,
Sway that this man, opon a day
Wyttles waned and wentt away— 540
Bott God wald noght þat he ware shente!

Ubi fregit tibiam.

In wodde vnwarly als he wentte,
Wyth a boghe hys bayn he brake,

St. Robert of Knaresborough

And þare lay Yue styll in a slake,
And weped iwysse and was full way; 545
The fende was fayn þat was hys fay.
Bott Robertt be reuelacioun
Was talde þis tribulacioun.
Robertt rayse, busked hym belyue,
And ranne to he come vnto Yue; 550
And when he saw hym sytt and say,
'Allas! allas!' and 'Waloway!'
Roberd badde hym be in rest—
To mane bowes all thinges for hys beste.

f. 51ᵛ He toke hys fotte and badde hym stand 555

Hic Robertus sanavit tibiam.

And blyssed ytt blythly wyth hys hand,
And ytt was hayll, na hurtt ytt had,
And than was Yue in gast full glad.
Agayne þan wentt thay bath in fere
And lyued togedir full many ȝhere. 560
In frost and snawe to Yorke he yode

Quomodo nudis pedibus ivit Eboracum.

Barefotte, þat men myght trace his blode,
Almos to purchace to hys pore;
Euer off catyffes hade he cure.
On theffes þan vengiaunce doune gun lyght 565
Þat robbed Sayntt Roberd on a nyght,
Brekand the chapell of Sayntt Hylde.
Sway sall robbers be begyled;
That gode men greues, þai sall hym gryme;
Yff ytt be taryed, ytt commes a tyme! 570

Quomodo vaccam domavit.

Off a myracle wyll I melle
Þat I trow be trew and lele.
Off Sayntt Robertt, anes as I rede,
Off a cow he had nede

gj [?] *in lower margin, f. 51, in later hand*

To hys pormen in hys place; 575
þareffor to the Erll Roberd gayse
And for a cowe he com and craued.
He graunte hym ane þat wytles raued.
He bad hym to hys forest fare
And 'Slyke a cowe take the þare. 580
I halde hir wyld; maik þou hyr tame.
To thi pore men lede hyr hame.'
Roberd rayked and þider yode
And fand this cowe, wyttles and wod;
Styll sho stode, nathynge stirrand. 585
Roberd arest hyr in a band
And hame wyth hyr full fast he hyed—
Meruayle them thoght þat stod besyde.
Byrde and best all bowed hym tyll,
Euer to wyrke aftir hys wyll. 590
Bott ȝytt a mare ferly befell
By this cow þat I sall telle.
A mane þare stode and sawe þis syght:
To the Erlle he hyed and spake on heght;
'Syr,' he sayd, 'sone sall ȝe se 595

Quomodo fautori eam donavit.

Ȝond kowe þat he sall gyff hyr me;
Wyth somme sotell trape or trayne
I sall gett ȝond kowe agayne.'
The Erle sayd, 'So motte I the,
Nay counsaylle þarto gyffe I the.' 600
This faytour forged hym on a wyle
Sayntt Robertt how he myght begylle.
He wapped hym in a wreched wede,
Schappen and sewed in many a screde,
Bygane to haltt, to grayn, to grett, 605
Sway Sayntt Robertt forto mett.
He cryed als a cayteyff chached in care,

596 *It may have been intended that the capital letter used for the first line of a new section should come at the beginning of this line, since in the margin there is a red mark beside the* ȝ

St. Robert of Knaresborough

Reuffully to rupe and to rare.
He cryed and craued Sayntt Robertt kowe:
'Roberd,' he sayd, 'grauntt me hyr nowe, 610
For his sake that sakles was salde;
Þoue sees I am bath croked and alde.'
Roberd sayd, 'Þou schapes þi skorne:
God gaffe, Gode haue! Taike hir by the horne
And lede hyr wyth the now away.' 615
Bott whatt byfell I thynk to say.
A fott this faytoure myght noght fle,
In lyme and lyth so halted he;
This wreke when he saw opon hym fall,
Opon Sayntt Robertt fast gun he call: 620
'Roberd,' he sayd, 'thou rewe on me!
This greuouse gylte forgyff þou me.'
Roberd said, 'Here may þou se
He that begyles, begylde sall be.'
He blyssed hys bane and mayd yt haile; 625
Þane hame he wentt and tald þis taile.

Quomodo cervos includebat orrio.

Off another wyll I neuen—
Wyth helpe of hyme þatt ys in heuen—
Off this forsayd þat I fynde;
Es noght to hyd ne halde behynd. 630
f. 53   Hertes full heghe of hede and horn
Vsed to comme to Robertt corn.
In feild thei fulled ytt wyth þare fette
And stroede ytt bath by sty and strette.
Whene Robertt wyst, he was noght payd, 635
Bott yode vnto þair lorde and sayd,
'Sir, thy catell euen and morne
Bathe distroes my hay and my corne.
Sir, gare kepe þaim, I the praye;
My gode es all in corn and hay 640
To my lyfelade þat I haue,
And to my cayteyffes in my caue.'
Than to Saintt Robertt he sayd,

St. Robert of Knaresborough

'Off thi harme I am noght payed;
Iff my catell do the skathe,   645
I gyffe the gode leue in thi lathe
To pynde my dere þare all bedeyn
To the tyme þat all þi harmes be seyne.'
Vnto this sawe Roberd assentt
And hame full wysely ys he wentt;   650
Bott he rayse vp oppon the morne
And fand þese hertys all in hys corne.
He wentt and wagged att them a wand
And draffe þise dere hame wyth hys hand,
And by law pynde þaime in hys lathe   655
And bade the lord gar se hys skathe.
Bott when þat knyght knewe wele þis case
Full mekyll meruayll in hertt he hayse;
'Robertt,' he sayd, 'þis ys enoghe!
Gar putt þir hertes in thi ploghe   660
And latt them drawe whyls þai may dre:
I grauntt þaim frely nowe to the.'
'Gramarcy, sir,' gun Robertt say,
And hyed hym hame by the redy way.

Quomodo cervos aratro copulavit.

Into hys ploghe he gartt þaim passe.   665
Als meke and mylde als lamme þai was
To dryff, to drawe, to louse, to bynde,
Als any ox þat man myght fynde.
All men had meruaille of this syght,
Sayd Roberd was a man of myght.   670
Thay loued our Lord omnipotentte
Sway great a grace þat hym had sente.

Quomodo demon apparuit ei.

The fend to man þat ys enmy
To Robertt had greatt inuy;
Als wreth he wex als a wype: 675
He thoghte to teyne hym wyth a type.
Apon a tyme, als I am lered,

St. Robert of Knaresborough

  Þe fend to Sayntt Robertt appered.
  In a lyknes blake and lathe—
  Ytt to discryffe I am noght grathe!   680
f. 54   Aboutte hys house þis harlott hyede,
  Hys deuociouns he defyed;
  All the vessell þat he fand
  He tyfeld and touched þaim wyth hys hand,
  His pott, hys panne, his sause, his soule,   685
  Wyth hys fyngers fatt and foule.
  When Robertt sawe, þat reken was,
  'A! wrech,' he sayd, 'I byde the pas
  Outte off this place now wyth thi playntte.
  Þou sall noght take me wyth a tayntt.'   690

Item alia vice demon apparuit ei.

  Another tyme, als I here tell,
  This noyand nedder fals and fell
  Appered in lyknes of a carle,
  Blake als pyke, bygan to parle.
  He toke a strenkell þare ytt stode   695
  Wyth haly watter gayn and gode,
  And wyth a wanyng of þat wate
  He gartt Sir Gerrard ga hys gate.

Item alias apparuit ei demon.

  Another tyme opon a nyghte,
  Roberd prayand for hys plyghte,   700
  In lyknes of a yonge chylde
  Off seuen ȝeres, meke and mylde,
  Appered and kneled opon hys kne
  And mowed befor Saynt Roberd ee;
  He mayd great noyse and great vnreste   705
f. 54ᵛ   To lett hym of hys praers preste.
  Bott Roberd sesed noght for þis syght,
  Bott euer prayand lay þat nyght.

679–80. *The first word in each line is almost illegible, and can be made out only with great difficulty*   682. deuociouns: *MS.* douociouns

Than þat warlow wex full way: \
Togedir he gedird all the stray 710 \
Wythin the place, and þane he paste \
Apon a fyer ytt forto caste. \
Than Robertt crossed ytt all aboutte \
And sone þat flamme was slokkend oute.

Item apparuit Roberto.

Another tyme þis Gerrard gryme 715 \
In lyknes transfigured hyme \
Off a chyld off sexten ȝhere \
Sway to Robertt to appere, \
And, on hym gapand, gyrned and gnaste; \
Robertt þaroff was noght abaste 720 \
And wyth hys staffe, als he was wontt, \
Bett hym and began to shontt. \
'Allas! allas!' begane to say, \
'I weynd. I weynd, full waloway! \
Yff I be slegh, I am ouersett 725 \
Off this rusty Robynett.' \
Thus Sathanas on ylkay syde \
Vmbeseged hym tyme and tyde \
In temptacions ilkane sere \
Þat may be wroght or wretyn here, 730 \
Sway to brynge hyme vnto baille, \
Bott of hys hertt he was sway haille \
That na fandyng myght hym fell— \
And that forthoght the fend of hell!

Quomodo Johannes rex ministravit Robertum.

Forthirmare now wyll I flytte 735 \
To enforme youe of a fytte, \
Kynge Johanne how Syr Bryane broght; \
Hys celle to se he him besoght. \
Robert he fand kneland prayand, \
Hys orysons contynuand, 740 \
That for nay noyse þat þai couth maike

714. flamme: *MS.* flamne

St. Robert of Knaresborough

Nay mare he mowed þan dose ane ake.
Þan Bryan sayd, wythouten lytte,
'Roberd, my brothir, rise vpe tyte.
Here standes our comly kyng wyth croune 745
To visett the wyth deuocioune.'
Þane Roberd rase full hastely
And spak to Bryan besily
And sayd, wythouten taryinge,
'Kenne me, Bryan, to my kynge.' 750
Sir Bryan sayd to hym by signe,
'Þis ys Kyng Johann maste condigne.'
Þan Robertt toke ane ere of corne
And sayd, standand the kyng byforne,

f. 55ᵛ   *De spica grani.*

'Yff thou be kynge, sir, kan þou oght 755
Off corn maike slyke ane ere of noght?'
Than þai sayd to that suffraynge,
'Þis man ys noght haille of brayne;
By this ensample þat we se
He schewes hymselffe a fole to be.' 760
'Sir,' he sayd, 'so motte I the,
Þis man ys mare wyse þane we,
For he serues bath day and houre
Na suffrayne botte hys Sauioure
In whame ys all wysdom & wytte; 765
This man full wysely folowes ytt.'
Than sayd the kyng, semly in saylle,
Vnto þis man spirituaylle,
'Aske me, Robertt, what þou wyll,
And godely sall I grauntte þaretyll.' 770
Tha⟨n⟩ sayd Robertt to the kynge,
'I haue nay nede of erthly thynge.
Enoghe I haue, syr, graunte mercy.'
Than wentt the kyng to hys company.

757–74. Thomas Flemyng   F F A   Thomas Flemyng .. Thi Em *in later hand in inner margin*   765. yll *deleted and expuncted before* ys.

Quomodo Yvo obiurgavit Robertum.

When the kyng was wentt, to hym come Yue 775
And sayd, 'Robertt, þoue wyll nott thryue.
Off the kyng why wald þou craue na gode,
Ne aske nay almos or he yode,
To þi poralles in this place?'
Roberd sayd, 'In Gode ys grace, 780
That godely gyffes vs kow and corne.'
'Yha,' quod Yue, 'bott noght by the horne!
Fole, gay furth, pursue þi frende.'
Roberd sayd, 'Yha,' and furth gan weynd

Quomodo rex dedit terram & cetera.

And to the kyng began to say, 785
'Certes, syr, I forgat to pray
For som almos, flesshe or fysshe.'
The kynge answerd and sayd, 'Iwysse,
I gyff and grauntt, est and west,
Als mekyll land in my forest 790
Als thou may tyll the wyth a ploghe.'
'Syr,' sayd Roberd, 'þat ys enoghe
Me to manteyn and my men.'
Agayn Sayntt Robertt rayked hym then.
Sirres, forsoth my hertt in sonder 795
Me thynke bath wepes and wirkes for wondir
That he, þat was sway waike a thynge,
Durst spek sway saffly wyth hys kynge.
Tyrauntes trembled þat did hym teyne;
Slyke selcouth was bath schewed and seyne. 800
Bestes and birdes vnto hym bowed;
Fendys hym fledde þat come in clowde;
Durste nayne hym dere he was so digne;
God for hym schewed full many signe.
Þan Robertt tilled and mayd hym toghe 805
Aboutte housebandry of hys ploghe.

Wether I do onn in *in later hand in lower margin, f.* 55ᵛ   782–92. *Marks
in later hand in outer margin*   787. r *in or* is *not distinct; it seems as
though another letter, which looks like* f, *has been written underneath; since in
this phrase* or *is the word usually used,* r *is to be preferred here*   Lower
margin, f. 56, And B [?] tho. wyffe *in later hand*

St. Robert of Knaresborough

Quomodo rector de Knaresburgo decimas exigebat.

Off Knaresburghe kyrke the persone þan
Rodely vnto Roberd ranne,
Hys teynde to craue of corne and hay,
Bott defyed hym wyth 'Nay'.   810
The persone sayd, 'Þou sall ytt gyffe,
Wyll þoue, nyll þoue, and I lyffe,
And I my happe haue and my hele;
The lawe sall ytt discusse and dele.'
Robertt sayd, 'Sothly þou raues   815
Þat vntrewly teyndes craues
To pore men þat appropird ys.
Neuer ȝytt yt newed to now a cresse!
My teyndes thou craues vnconnandly;
I graunte the Crystys cursynge forthi!'   820
T⟨h⟩e persone tonge, þat toyled þis sayntt
And displesed hym wyth hys playntt,
Was wyth vengiaunce and wyth wreke
Spoyled þat he myght neuer speke,
Ne had nay space, bott att hys laste   825
In payne and pouertt hethen he paste.
Thus he þat couettys thyng vnlele,
When he deghes hais noght to dele
Off hys aghen wythin hys wane.
Yll gytten gode, men says ytt sall be gane.   830

Quomodo habuit spiritum prophecie.

Ȝitt of a meruayle list me mele,
That I trowe be trewe and lele,
Off Roberd that was resonable
And to pore men profytable,
How Bryan, by the kyngys commaundment,   835
Into this North þat tym was sentt;
Bott on nay wyse wald he weynd
Bott by Sayntt Robertt hys faythfull freynd.

f. 57

817. In appropird *the first* r *is unlike any other* r *in the manuscript, but resembles no other letter, and* r *is obviously the letter required here*   829. place *expuncted before* wane

St. Robert of Knaresborough

Full ryally to hym he rayd
And kneland on hys kne he sayd,   840
'I beseke the for me pray
And blysse me or I weynd away.'
Roberd badde Sir Bryane stand
And blythely blyssed hym wyth hys hand,
Spekan to hym in prophecy,   845
'Weynd þoue worschipfully;
Gouerne þou sall well þi degre
In ioy and in prosperite,
Bott agayn commes þou nay mare.
Cryst he kepe the nowe fray care!'   850

f. 57ᵛ   Þir wordes when Bryan vnderstod
Away he wentt wyth drery mod,
And to Northe Cuntre he rayd,
And þair he dyed als Robertt sayd;
His saule passed vnto paradyse   855
For in this warld Bryan was wyse.
Here may ȝe se, bath yonge and alde,
A prophett þat he may be called.

Quomodo prophetavit de Fontinensibus.

Bott ȝytt forthermare I fynd—
Þat ys noght gode to hald behynd—   860
Eftsones how he prophetised:
Þase wordes to wrytt I am avised.
Befor Robertt that ryghtwyse was
Outt off this wreched dayle suld passe,
'When I am sweltt,' he sayd to somme,   865
'Monkes of Fountaunce sammenn sall comme
My body forto bere away
Beried to be in thare abbay.
Ytt ys my wyll wyth myght and mayn
Stalworthly þat ȝe stand agayn.   870
I wyll be doluen wharso I deghe;
Beried my body þare sall ytt be;

860. noght: o *interlined*

St. Robert of Knaresborough

  Wythouten end here wyll I rest;
  Here my wounyng chese I fyrste,
f. 58 Here wyll I leynd, her wyll I ly   875
  In this place perpetuely.'
  Roberd keped a ryghtwyse reule
  All tym þat he couth crepe or creule,
  In crage, in creues, or in caue,
  Sway sadde he was hys saule to saue.   880
  Fray sted to sted he stepped and stode
  Þar nay myscheffe merred hys mode;
  Comforth ne care, baile ne blysse,
  Myght noght chaunge hys chere a rysshe;
  Durese, dishese, dere ne dred,   885
  Well ne wyrschipe, als I red,
  Myght stire hym halffe a stryde;
  All bytternes he couth abyde;
  Forthi our Lord to lerred and lewed
  Many ferly for hym schewed,   890
  Hys godnes bath to gloryfy
  And vther men to edyfy,
  And als to men hys mekyll myght
  Forto mostre day and nyght,
  Myracles sway many wythouten maike 895
  Our Sauiour schewed has for hys saike,
  Bath efter ded and in hys lyffe—
  The halff þat I kane noght discryffe.
  Thus in romaunce haue I herd
f. 58ᵛ That Roberd rouled hys lyffe in werlde. 900
  To hym be louynge lastand ay
  Þat hym gaffe power forto pray,
  And forto saue oure saules syne
  In blysse bringand fra bitter pyne.
  Than Roberd, aye þat ryghtwys wasse, 905
  Persayued þat hym bode hethen passe
  By dede, þat nouther duke ne kynge
  Ne suffrayn sparys he; nay thinge

891. *MS.* bath bath *with second* bath *expuncted*   900. hys:
MS. lys

Sinfull ne saint, ryche ne pore,
May sayff ne maike nane, sound ne sore. 910
Quomodo ornavit lampidem suam ante mortem.
He sett hym sadly forto say
Psalmes and ympnes, and forto pray
To Gode and to hys Moder dere,
And to all hys sainttys sere,
And to hys aungels and all 915
Doune to comme began to call,
Att hys wey⟨n⟩dynge hym to wyshe
And to bryng hys saule to blesse.
Þan in seknes sadde and sare
He fell þat he myght moue nay mare, 920
Bott cryed on Gode contynuely,
'Lord, on me þou haue mercy!'
When Yue saw Roberd draw to dede
Full wille he wex þan off hys rede;

f. 59 *De Yvonis doloribus et gemitu.*
He syghed, he sobbed and gaffe hym yll, 925
Bott ay badde Robertt Yue be styll;
In hertt was heuy all þat herde
Þat Robertt weynd suld off þis werlde.
Kneland þai come and þaim commend,
Þar saules to saue wythouten end. 930
Than monkes of Fountaunce come full tyte
And wyth þaim broght an habytt whytt,
And sayd, 'Robertt, this sall þou haue
Wyth the when thou gase to thi graffe.'
Roberd sayd, 'Sirres, when I deghe 935
My aghen clethyng suffyce to me.'
(Bott ȝytt they dyd when he was ded
Befor that myght noght stand in sted;
Þat ys to say, in coule hym cled,
And sway thay bare Robertt to bed.) 940
When Robertt saw þat he suld dee
'In manus tuas, Domine,'

Catchwords he syghed *at right-hand side of lower margin, f.* 58ᵛ
942. *These words are in the same kind of writing as much of the Latin*

St. Robert of Knaresborough 71

He sayd and sweltt and gaffe hys gaste
To the Fader and þe Son and the Haly Gaste.
Than aungels broght hys saull to blysse,   945
Honored it to be als ane off hys.
Yue closed hys eghe wyth mekyll care;
All wepid for way, bath lesse and mare.
A herce they sett sone apon trees
f. 59ᵛ   And dyd deuoutly dirigees.   950
When thys was talde, Fountaunce full faste
Wyth great power þider paste
To reue þaim Robertt body blyste,
Bott Knaresburgh of tham wyste,
Off men off armes araed routte   955
Forto hald þase monkes oute.
Wythouten harme so hyed they hame;
Bare nane for hys body blayme.
Than caryed and com outt of the cuntree
Mane and wyff of all degree,   960
Pore and rych, all maide þaim boune
Wyth men off religyoune,
To bere hys body oponn a bere
Wyth melody þat men myght here,
And beryed hym in a grayff full god   965
In the chapell þat was of the Haly Rode,
Befor the heghe awter in a toumbe;
Hys myracles may nay man soumbe
In the chapell—þat er red full ryffe—
That Walter wroght hym in hys lyffe.   970
All þat was seke and to hym soght,
Be þat thai yode, þaim ayled noght.
Crased & croked, bath deiff and domme,
War cured þat to hys toumbe wald comme.
Þe halt was heled, the lame was lyght,   975
f. 60   Blynde and bysen hadde þair syght,
Men of menbirs þat war mayned

section-headings, which tends to be slightly different from the rest. There is also a line drawn below and above the writing
  Lower margin, f. 59ᵛ, bryan flemyng in later hand

Was saued full sound when þai wer saynd;
Obcessed off fend he gart þaim flytte,
Wytles and wod won in þair wytt; 980
Lunatykes and frenesyse
Thrugh hys myght ware mayd full wyse;
Baran bare hir childe belyffe
And some ware rased fra ded to lyffe.
And, to conclude þaim all in fere, 985
All þat hurtt hadde any here,
Or any seknes, all ware saued
Thayr hele because þai of hym craued.
Þai may be glad and blyth þat has
Slyke a patrone off þair place 990
Þat ys off power forto pray
For thare plyght bath nyght & day.
God for hys saike hys seruaundes saues,
Nathyng denyes hym þat he craues.
All praers þus for þar place 995
To God to gouern þaim by grace,
And whaso greues god men þerin
Or payres þair place, þai do great syn
And er acursed by bulles sere
Þat Papys of Rome has graunt þaim here. 1000
Forthi I rede you all forbere
Sanctuaries to do þaim dere.
Yue ledde hys lyff lang in that sted
Aftur the tyme Roberd was ded
In bedes, praers, and orisounes 1005
And in othir deuociounes.
Þan dyed þis daynty man a-day
And went to ioye þat last sall ay,
To the whike he bryng yow all and me,
Amen, Amen per charite. 1010

DE INITIO CREACIONIS ORDINIS SANCTE TRINITATIS

Almyghty Lord in mageste
Þat was and ys and ay sall be,

1008. went to: *MS.* wentt o

St. Robert of Knaresborough

  Grauntte me nowe and euermore
  Þe grace þat I besoght before.
  Eftyr the tyme Roberd was dede   1015
  Yue wouned styll in þatt stede,
  Apperand in perfeccioune
  To serue God in subieccioune.
  The place wyth the appurtinaunce
f. 61   Tha⟨n⟩ gyffen was to hys gouernaunce;   1020
  He gaff ytt—ȝytt all men may se—
  To Couerham wyth a charter fre,
  Þair to fynd perpetuely
  Tway chanons syngand sykyrly;
  And sway thay dyd ȝheres diuerse,   1025
  Bott clerly kanne I noght reherce
  How ytt wentt outt off þair hand,
  Bott trewly als I vndyrstand
  That ytt some tyme stode desolatte
  For dede or elles for some debaytte,   1030
  And sway entird ay to be
  The Ordir of the Haly Trinite.
  In ane hede persons thre ar knytt;
  By þis ensaumpill sall þou wytt
  Playnly þat possessiounes   1035
  Off this ryall relygiounes
  Deuised and deltt sall be in thre:
  Tway partes to the Ministre and his menȝhe;
  Þe third þat raysed ys of þar rentt
  To the Haly Land sall ytt be sentt   1040
  To releue and to relese
  Crysten men þat ar in dishese,
f. 61ᵛ   Ys doune in full depe doungeouns
  Pyned in pyttes and i prisouns
  Omong the Jewes, and Saraȝyns   1045
  In þair fetters fast þaim byndys
  And in þair ploghes puttys þaim to draw
  And sithen þair sede settes þaim to sawe.
  The third porcion of this ordir fre,

1015. was: *MS.* wad   1022. *Cross in later hand in outer margin*

Þat þai send byȝond the se, 1050
Ys raunsoun and redempcioun
Off ylkay a crysten region,
Crysten cayteffys forto by
Outt of prysouns þair þai ly.
Mynistre þus expounde ȝhe may, 1055
Þat ys bott seruaund forto say;
All yff he serue, ȝytt hys degre
Als a prelate awe to be.
Þis worde ys wreten of our Lord,
Þat to þis curate may accorde. 1060

Non veni ministrari sed ministrare.

Oure Sauiour sais, yff ytt be soghte,
'Her to be serued come I noght,
Bott forto serue I come myselff.'
Þis same he schewed vnto twelff.
The clethinge of þise men perfyte 1065
By this incheson ytt ys whit:
For the angels bryght þat lyghted lawe
In clething whytt als any snaw
Bysyde the graue of our Sauiour,
And also by thys same coloure 1070
May men vndirstand and se
The clennes of mannes chastite;
The crosse, þat on þair clethinge cleues,
Ys mynd of the rode þat man releues—
The rede by resoun of hys blode, 1075
Þe blewe for the water þat wyth ytt yode:
Thus I vndirstand þaim here.

Tot capita tot sentencie.

Ilke hede has a sentence sere
How the Order of the Haly Trinite
First begane—here sall ȝe se; 1080
Als I haue herd I vndirtoke,
Bott I haue ooyn ytt in nay boke
Off twa heremites haue I herd

St. Robert of Knaresborough 75

That wyse ware when þai woned in werld;
Off the Haly Gast þai wair inspired, 1085
Bott anely Gode noght þai desyred.
A preciouse purpos ayther toke
And wysely wrayt ytt in a boke;
To the Pape þay putt þat blyssed byll
And he resaued ytt wyth gode wyll. 1090
When he hade þair gud intentt
Wyth thar byll away he wentt,
Prayand God to schewe hym sone
By þat byll what suld be doyne,
f. 62ᵛ And called hys counsayll in this case 1095
To beseke God off hys grace.
Bott aftur what befell
Forre þair prayers sall I tell.
The Pape als he sang messe a-day
Specially for þis case to pray, 1100
Appered ane aungell bryght of ble
And kest a clething att hys kne,
And badde hym take þat clething tyte
Þairin to cleth hym men perfyte.
The Pape doune falland wyth hys handes 1105
Loued our Lord þat hys seruaundes
Sway saues and comforthes ay
And grauntes all þaim þat þai for pray.
He toke this clethinge cleyn and whyte
And þarein cledde þase heremytes tyte, 1110
Badde þaime increse and multyply
Here to lyffe a halely.
Þan þai stepped ouer streme and strand
And releued in the Haly Land;
Cayteffes þat wer chached in care, 1115
Pressed in prisouns, naked and bare,
Plonged in ploghe, in cartt drawand,

1102. ken *expuncted before* kne   1102-3. Robert *in later hand upside down in inner margin.*   1108-9. Robert *in later hand upside down in inner margin*   1109. *In* cleyn *the letters* cl *and* yn *are obvious, and what is visible of the other letter can be* e

Outt thei boght þaim wyth besand.
Þan þus began þe ordre fre
That ys off the Haly Trinite. 1120
Detbundon þis order ys to do
On this wise þase cayteffes to,
Thaim to raunsoune and to by
Wyth the third partt off thar tresory.
Nay mair att þis tym kan I say, 1125
Bott wyth all my hertt I pray
To God þat he þaim saue & send
To myrth þat neuer mare sall haue end. Explicit.

A PRAYER

Hayle! cheftane, Cristes aghen confessour,
Als seruauntt of our Sauiour; 1130
Haile! Saintt Robert, thrugh Goddes grace
Pere and patron of this place;
Haile! our gouernour and our gyde,
Haile! þat vs socoures on ylka syde,
Haile! þat couers our caytefte, 1135
Haile! þat saues þat serue wyll the,
Haile! Robert, þat ay ryghtwyse was,
Þi bred was menged ay wyth asse;
Haile! diamaunde, þat dose vs ese,
Fordo and dylle all our dishese. 1140
I beseke the to begyne
And to conuerte me fray my synne;
My lyppes wyth louynges be fuffylled,
Þi wyll to wyrke þat I be wylled.
For þe grace to the þat graunted was 1145
Þe bandes þou brest of my tryspas,
And owtt of prison, I the pray,
Off synne my saulle gar wynne away.

1134. *Though the last letter of* socoures *is not plain, what is visible can belong to* s, *and the present tense of the verb, found in* couers 1135 *and* saues 1136, *is appropriate here* 1133-4. Thomas . . . emy . . . *in later hand upside down* 1136-7. And *in later hand upside down in outer margin* 1147. *Between* o *and* w *of* owtt *there is a letter which cannot be read; it may be a* w *which was spoilt as written and so repeated*

St. Robert of Knaresborough

Lede me, Roberd, outt of luste,
For all my doynges ar bott duste.   1150
Weile I waytt, wythowten weyn,
My synnes to schew or to be seyn
Are sulped as sute ys in my syght;
Þarfor my lyffe may noght be lyght.
A! blyssed saint and cetiȝand,   1155
In heuen þat shynes als diamaund,
Dresse me fra dampnacion
And send me saluacion.
When I am couped, I pray the come
To defend me at þat dome   1160
Þat the feynd sall fourme for my foly,
Þat I may weynd wyth victory
Wyth the to woune in endles blysse.
Ryghtwys Roberd, pray for þis! Amen.
Explicit.

f. 35ᵛ   ORACIO PRESIDENTIS

Hayle! Saint Robert, a confessoure   1165
Þate suetely serued oure Sauioure;
Hayle! peirles patrone of þis place,
I besek the send vs grace,
Strenght and myght—þat wounes herin—
The to serue wythouten syne,   1170
And wyth our seruice þat we maye
Her perfytely please the aye,

f. 36   And helpe vs i necessite
Sen þou arte our avowe fre
And saint on whayme mast tryst we haue,   1175
This house and vs to kepe and saue
Fray dett and dedlye synnes seuenn,
And forto bryng vure saules to heuenn;
And of thi godenes graunt me grace
Sway ryghtwislye to reul this place,   1180

1155. b *in later hand in inner margin*   1159. the *is difficult to make out*   *Lower margin, f.* 63ᵛ, s . . te Robert is my . . . . and it [?] . emy . . nd *in later hand upside down*

And sway to gouernn to my degre
Þat I, all yff I simple be,
Occupyes als presidentt
By grace þat God here has me sentt—
May be vnto the saluacioun   1185
Off all this congregacioun,
And hape and helefull mayntenaunce
Off the place for my gouernaunce—
And helpe to me in all my nede
And sauyng to my saule and mede;   1190
And suffrandly, I the beseke,
Of maners to be myld and meke,
In persecuciounes pacientt
And in myne office diligentt—
My malicoly thou amese   1195
And comfurthe me in all dishese—
And sway tholemode of my thoght
That ire ne wrath ouersett me noght;
And boxum to euiralkay ded
Þat may multiply my mede;   1200
Of thoght and dede forto be chaste
And mercyfull þou make me maste,
And to be abstinentt at borde
And trew and lele to be of worde
And sobyr whene I am assayled—   1205
And send me helpe þat neuer fayled—
And compacientt forto be
Of all in anger þat I se.
Forgyffnes gett me of my syne
And of my mysded gar me mynne—   1210
And forto vse all vertues ilkay day,
And of all vices to voyde away—
And victorye of this warld als
Off my fleshe and the feinde fals—
And stythe bath well & way to drye.   1215
Als ane of thine þoue socoure me
And all my brether, lered and lewed,

1202-3. And *in later hand in inner margin*

And my systers, seryne or shwed;
In charyte generalle
Haue mercy, Roberd, of thayme alle; 1220
Helpe me to kepe myne obseruaunce,
And, sen I haue the gouernaunce
By elecciōn of this place,
I beseke the send me grace
To gouernn ytt in prosperyte 1225
That ytt to the lele louyng be,
To hym þat hyrd ys of this shepe
Þat I haue cure of forto kepe,
And to hys Moder free
And to all hys halowes he; 1230
And to my felaghes mare and lesse
Helpe and hele and halynes,
And bath of saule and body blysse
And saluacion aftyr this;
And graunt me myght, strengh and grace, 1235
Þair simple prelate of this place,
With discrecion that I maye
Sway gouernn ytt bath nyght and day,
And Goddes seruice wyth instance
And all vther obseruaunce, 1240
In pece, in quiete, and i reste
And in charete þat ys beste,
By meke sufferaunce & pacience
Þat, for my dughty diligence,
When I am ded and doluenn lyse 1245
Tha⟨t⟩ I may passe to paradyse,
And att þase fre yhates wyth the mette
And here thi voce þat ys so swette
To me sayand on this wyse,
'Welcom vnto paradyse. 1250
Welcom, son, vnto this place,
For sen þou hase thrugh grace

Inner margin, f. 36ᵛ, And Thomas Flemynge *and other marks and separate letters in later hand vertically*   1224–6. I beseke the send me grace *in later hand in outer margin*

Well gouerned thi lytyll cell,
Wythowten end here sall þou dwell
In joy and solace and in blysse.'   1255
Saintt Robertt, thou grauntt me this,
And helpe þus þat ytt may be.
Amen, Amen per charite.

ORACIO AD BEATUM ROBERTUM

Hayle! heremete mast þat ys of myght
Fray way to were the wafull wyght.   1260
Hayle! in care þat comforthes all
That hertely her wyll on the call.
Hayle! man þat was wythowten make,
I beseke the, for hys sake
Here þat nathinge the denied   1265
Þat þoue aftur craued or cryed,
For this grett prerogatyff
Fray langor lese me; of my lyffe
I beseke the saue me sound,
Whider or whare or when I found,   1270
On land or water wheder yt be;
Fra all greuaunce of aduersite,
Saintt Robertt, kepe me I the pray,
Fra thonour and leuenyng ylka day,

f. 38   Fray sodann ded and dremes,   1275
And fray all dishesse þat es
Of fier, of water or of wound,
Or any greuaunce of this ground,
Fray fendes fals and fell
And men þat keyn ar and crowell,   1280
Fray wyld bestes and enposynnyng
And vermyn and all vther thyng,
Fra bytyng, thretyng, and fray theffys,
And all maner of myscheffys
That outher may me greff or skath   1285
In saule, in body or in bath;

1253–5. mu [?] *in later hand vertically in outer margin*   1285. That:
MS. Tthat

St. Robert of Knaresborough

And fray vnhappes all that ar here,
Fray noye and ned and angers sere,
Fray tribulacion, traye and teyne,
An destany of cares keyn; 1290
Fray way and wandreth of þis werld—
Or wyth myscomforth to be merred—
Fray plyghtes and pareles manyfalde
Of hongyr, threst, myst or calde;
Fray pouerte and perplexite 1295
And combraunce of all catyefte;
Fray dole of passion and of pyne,
Fray fautes and all enseging syne,
Fray syte and fray all seknes here,

f. 38ᵛ Fray mournyng and all sorowes sere, 1300
Fray dett and fray all dedely syn
Off trispas, wikkednes I am in;
Fray vengeaunce, wreth and wrechednes,
And fray all pereles mare and lesse
Þat was or ys or may befall. 1305
Sayntt Robertt, kepe me fray thaym all,
And grauntt me, for thi charite,
When I am ded þat I may se
Thiselff wyth aungels stand me by
My countes to cast, and to reply 1310
Off my trispas ylkay playntte,
That I be noght tane wyth tayntte;
Bott fray þat bytter bayle gar brynge
My saule to se my semely Kynge
And euer to belde wyth hym in blysse— 1315
I beseke the grauntte me this. Amen. Explicit.

Lower margin, f. 38, Thomas in later hand upside down 1305. Þat:
MS. Þhat

NOTES

(For references to *Egert.*, *Har.*, *LVL.*, and *HT.* see Appendixes.)

1. The last word of the heading above this line is difficult to transcribe. The sign which follows *burg* is ꝑ which is elsewhere used as a contraction for *is* in Latin. Here the accusative is required after *iuxta*, so it has been expanded to *um*, the usual accusative form of the name in Latin works. Over the second *r* there is a sign like that normally used for the contraction of *ur*, but as this expansion is unnecessary it has been ignored. The original may have had a form *bğꝑ*, with the contraction mark above, and this has been retained even though the expansion has been made in the copy.

9. *Yraell.* Although *OED.* cites one example of a similar spelling for 'Israel', it is most probable that the omission of *s* here is simply a scribal error.

17. *Saintt.* Although during the pontificate of Alexander III the right of canonization was regarded as reserved to the Holy See ('the formal legal establishment' of this right was settled by the Decretals of Gregory IX, 1234, according to E. W. Kemp in *Canonization and Authority in the Western Church* [Oxford, 1948], p. 107), yet the practice continued whereby a bishop's sanction led to local veneration. As there is no record of the official canonization of St. Robert of Knaresborough, it is most probable that he received only this episcopal beatification. According to the *Book of Saints* (compiled by the Benedictine monks of St. Augustine's Abbey, Ramsgate [London, 1939], p. 231), Robert's festival is celebrated on 14 May, and he is noted as one of those saints not included at the date of compilation in the *Roman Martyrology*, the official church register. In addition, *LVL.* 114 states that he was not canonized.

17–20. Interpret: 'Concerning St. Robert, that hermit who was shown here to be perfect, who shut himself up in a cave afar off in a cliff near Knaresborough', or '... perfect; he shut himself ....' Such pronominal omission is not uncommon; cf. 630, 703, 810, &c.

28. *by a boke.* The author is definite in wanting it to be believed that he was drawing on a written source. Cf. 94, 266, 282, 327, 899.

29. *frere.* Trinitarians are commonly referred to as 'friars', though, according to Professor Knowles (op. cit., p. 102), their way of life bore a much closer resemblance to that of the Augustinian, or Black, Canons. Probably here *frere* is not used in a specialized sense, and means no more than 'a member of a religious order', and this may be taken to be the meaning throughout. In the case of the Cistercian brother (101) it could not mean 'friar'.

30. *Fray Sayntt Robertys.* Whenever any reference is made to 'St. Robert's' in Papal Letters or in the edited volumes of State Papers, it is always the Trinitarian house at Knaresborough that is indicated, so this house is almost certainly meant by *Sayntt Robertys.* The church at Pannal is also dedicated to St. Robert as the advowson was granted to the house at Knaresborough (*Char. Rolls, 9 Ed. I,* m. 14 [*1257–1300,* p. 240]).

35. *Vhenn.* The initial letter could be transcribed as *U* since it does not resemble an ordinary *V,* but the same letter occurs on 134, and inside it there is a small *v*; in addition, initial *v/u* is always written as *v* in the text. The letter is also larger and more decorated than any other letter beginning a new paragraph; this may be because what follows is really the first paragraph of *M.,* since the preceding part is only the prologue.

fared. The last letter is unmistakably *d,* though the present tense would be preferable since that is the tense used in the following lines. An *s* could have been miscopied as *d* by the scribe. Interpret: 'have fared'.

39 ff. Cf. the *Prologue* to *Cursor Mundi* (ed. R. Morris [E.E.T.S. 1874–93]) which gives a list of the heroes concerning whom people enjoyed hearing romances; in Barbour's *Bruce* (ed. W. W. Skeat [E.E.T.S. 1870–99]), iii, ll. 435 ff., there is another example of the popularity of the reading aloud of romances. Similar lists of heroes are not uncommon in other Middle English poems.

45. *he.* The pronoun may be used here as a substantive meaning 'a man, person', but, on the other hand, *he* may represent a scribal error for *ȝhe* (for this spelling cf. 1055), the second personal pronoun plural, referring to *Fadir and Son and Haly Gaste.*

me. This may be the accusative of either the personal pronoun or the reflexive pronoun. In the former case the interpretation would be: 'But, Father, Son and Holy Ghost, do You speed me (in telling the story) of a better man.' In the latter case interpret: 'But, O Father, Son and Holy Ghost, may I hasten (*or* prosper) (in telling the story). . . .' In both these interpretations *he* has been considered as the correct reading, but if it is emended to *ȝhe,* then only the former of the two is likely.

49. *Toccus Flos.* Three of the Latin lives of St. Robert are in agreement about the name of the saint's father; *Egert.* reads *Tocco Flore* (ablative), *Har. Toccus Flos, LVL. Tok Flos.* Robert is given the surname *Koke* in *Chron. Lan.,* possibly through a scribal error, and further variations are found in unreliable accounts. *Toccus* no doubt corresponds to ON. *Tóki.* St. Robert's father is often reputed to have been Mayor of York; Drake (op. cit., p. 359) states that he occupied that position about 1195, though he does not show where he found that information. However, Farrer points out (op. cit., p. 178) that it seems

that not until 1213 were the king's writs addressed to 'the mayor and true men of York', and so in the case of Toccus Flos 'mayor' should be interpreted in a looser sense than the modern one, simply 'the chief citizen'.

51. *Suniuyte*. In the manuscript there is a spot over the first minim, but it does not look like the beginning of the line which usually indicates an *i*. *Egert.* reads *Siminima*, *Har. Sunniva*, and *LVL. Simima*. Attention need not be paid to other variations since they seem to be based on either *Egert.* or *Har.* The name was most probably ON. *Sunniva*, and a succession of minims is very liable to scribal corruption. In *Documents Illustrative of the Social and Economic History of the Danelaw*, ed. F. M. Stenton (London, 1920), p. 309, mention is made of *Henricus filius Sunniue*.

52. *Sho bare a barne* . . . . According to Leland (op. cit., p. 86) Robert was the eldest son, and thus forfeited his inheritance when he took up the religious life, but Leland cites no source for this information. Cf., however, *LVL.* 45, *Nil curans hereditatem*.

53. *Robertt . . . thei named hym*. Several saints bore this name, e.g. Robert, the founder of the Cistercian Order, who died in 1098, and Robert of Newminster, one of the founders of Fountains Abbey, and later Abbot of Newminster (see also note to 89), and others who are listed in the *Book of Saints (ut sup.)*, p. 231.

All this passage is a fairly free rendering of the corresponding account of *Egert.* 1 of Robert's childhood and youth; both endeavour to show that even at that early stage he gave proof of his godly character, but whereas *Egert.* is content with describing it in the abstract, apart from mentioning that he frequented churches and monasteries, *M.* prefers more concrete examples, such as 69–70, 77–79, 81–82.

75–76. As there is an *a* after 75 in the manuscript and after 76 a *b*, probably to indicate the lines should be transposed, this has been carried out since they then make better sense. Interpret: '. . . and of all virtues more diverse by half than (those) I can tell you of here.'

89 ff. Two writers, Gent (op. cit., p. 259) and Hargrove (op. cit., p. 90), state that Robert had previously been a monk at Whitby. Hargrove also adds that he was at Fountains and later became Abbot of Newminster, whilst Gent keeps the correct account, given in *M*.

97 ff. The mistake they have made is caused by the fact that there was another Robert, generally known as Robert of Newminster, also a Yorkshireman—from the Craven district—who was a monk at Whitby and Fountains, and who became the first Abbot of Newminster which he helped to found. This Robert died about the middle of the twelfth century.

92. *phannoune*. Since the ending of the word (< Fr. *fanon*) as it stands in the manuscript does not rhyme with *boune*, it has been

Notes

emended to *oune*. The *phannoune* is the fanon or maniple used by a cleric in major orders.

93–96. Cf. *Egert.* 1, '. . . sed quid eum ab hoc incepto proposito retraxit, penitus ignoro. Ergo Deo totum committimus, cui nullum latet secretum, melius quam nostris ignoranciis aliquid temere diffinire.'

98. *page*. If this really means 'boy' it seems to have been included purely for the sake of rhythm and alliteration, since there is no mention of Robert's having been accompanied by someone else in any of the Latin accounts, nor is the boy mentioned again in *M*.

99. According to *Egert.* 2 Robert *occidentales secessit in partes* to reach Newminster, which seems a very roundabout way. (See also the notes to 405 and 836.) The comparisons between *M.* and *Egert.* at these points may lend support to the thesis that the author of *M.* was a Northcountryman (see Introduction, pp. 26–27). If the direction in the common original of *M.* and *Egert.* (see Introduction, p. 32) were similar to that given in *Egert.*, and if the author of *M.* were a Northcountryman, what would be more natural than that, knowing more about northern geography, he corrected the directions that he found in his source, since it would appear strange to him—as to any Northerner—that Robert should have gone westwards from York to reach Newminster in Northumberland? On the other hand, if the direction in the common original were similar to that given in *M.*, then a northern author of *M.* would tend to preserve such a direction, whereas the author of *Egert.*, or one of his predecessors, has altered it for some reason. It is not to be denied that the alteration—or preservation—found in *M.* should perhaps be also attributed to an earlier author, but, since the dialect of the author of *M.* is obviously Northern, it is most probable that he himself was responsible.

100. *Newmostres*. Newminster, a Cistercian monastery near Morpeth in Northumberland.

113 ff. The most satisfactory interpretation of this passage is: 'So he, the head of that house, ruled him then through grace, while he (Robert) was engaging in extremely holy practices, fervently afflicting his body, and persevering both in prayers and penance and with steadfast endeavour.' For the interpretation of the present participle by 'while he was . . . ing', cf. 700.

125–6. Cf. *Egert.* 2, 'Quatuor mensibus et una quindena completis, Spiritu Sancto revelante . . .', but *Chron. Lan.* (p. 25) gives the length of his stay as *tres menses et dimidium*. In *Har.* 3 Robert is accused of apostasy by some men, nominally religious, after he has left 'the monastery', presumably Newminster, but he remains unperturbed.

126. *reued*. Judged by the context the word may mean 'dwelt, tarried', and it may be connected with OE. *ge-hrēfan*, 'to roof'.

127–8. According to *Egert.* 2 it was the Holy Spirit that told Robert to leave Newminster.

142. *tow(r)e.* The Roxburghe Club edition of *The Metrical Life of St. Robert of Knaresborough* prints this word as *cow(rte)*, but the first three letters are obviously *tow*; the last letter is *e*; the intervening letter has a tail and can well be an *r*. Cf. *towne* and *toure* 524.

143. *All had forsaken, chyld and wyffe.* Cf. *Egert.* 3 and *Har.* 4, *ad uxorem et filios.* A possible explanation of this difference is that 'children' would not have fitted into the line of *M*.

144. The reason for the knight's present life as a hermit is given in *Chron. Lan.*, and also in *Har.* 4, '. . . ut iram regis Ricardi, ob quandam offensam eius animam querentis, ad tempus declinaret, in habitu heremitico, ne a satellitibus regis agnosceretur'.

161–2. The reason for the hermit's flight is attributed to the devil in *Egert.* 3, but *Har.* 4 says that it was because Richard died, leaving him free from persecution: 'Habitaverunt itaque simul . . . donec rex Ricardus, lege mortis compellente, viam universe carnis ingrediens, mundo valefaceret. Rege igitur de medio sublato, . . . miles . . . ad uxorem et filios, ut canis ad vomitum, reversus est.' *Chron. Lan.* (pp. 25–26) agrees with *Har.* on this point. None of the Latin accounts states, as *M*. does (155–7), that the devil turned to the hermit because he could not overcome Robert. *M*. 153–60 correspond to only one phrase in *Egert.*, *instigante diabolo*.

163–4. Cf. Proverbs xxvi. 11 and 2 Peter ii. 22.

167–8. On considering *Egert.* 3, *Robertus solus remansit*, it appears that Robert did not remove to another cave, as *M*. seems to suggest, but returned to the one he had occupied with the hermit.

171. *ympnes.* It is unlikely that the manuscript reading *ympies* means 'little devils', modern 'imps', because OE. *impa/e* would not give such an ending; the OE. word meant 'young shoot, scion'. In addition, the word is not used in the sense 'imp' until the sixteenth century. It is more probable that the form is a mistake for *ympnes*, and the sense would be that after his temptations Robert glorified God by singing hymns.

174. *wydow.* *Har.* 5 gives her name as *Helena*, Gent (op. cit., p. 262) as *Philadelphia*. J. R. Walbran (op. cit., p. 167 n.) suggests that she was a Percy or a Plumpton; members of both these families lived in the neighbourhood.

178. *þe chapell . . . of Sayntt Hylde.* J. R. Walbran (op. cit., p. 167 n.) suggests that the stones used for the building of the Roman Catholic Chapel at Knaresborough were probably from the ruins of this chapel. He also states, together with Hargrove (op. cit., p. 90), that the names 'Chapel Field' and 'St. Hile's Nook' still survive there. The place is near Rudfarlington, formerly Rof- or Rough-, about two miles south of Knaresborough.

Notes 87

Har. 5 (p. 130) gives more details concerning the widow's gifts and the situation of the chapel: '. . . mulier . . . dedit ei ecclesiam Sancte Hilde in saltu de Knaresburgo constructam, ubi quondam villa grandis que Rothferlingtoun vocabatur a rege Stephano subversa refertur. De terra autem adiacente quantum ei fodere placuit concessit, et victui necessaria liberaliter impendit.'

181. *all.* The stroke through the word may be meant to cross it out, though it could be the usual stroke through *ll*, and the pen may have caught and splashed when making it. The metre does not show whether or not it should be omitted.

183–4. Cf. *Egert.* 3, *Robertus fere per annum . . . solus remanebat*, and *Har.* 5 (p. 130), *Habitavit . . . semotus a conturbacione hominum.* *M.* may mean essentially the same as the other two, for the *poralles* may have been only casual guests, the kind of people from whom he would not wish to cut himself off.

184. *poralles.* The word is generally used with reference to the poor as a class, and only rarely, as here, with reference to poor persons.

185. Cf. *Egert.* 4, '. . . dum vir Dei in oracionibus et aliis sacris meditacionibus immobilis pernoctavit . . . .' No indication of the time of the thieves' attack is supplied in *Har.*

186. *theffys.* None of the Latin accounts gives the number of thieves at this point, but in *Egert.* 14 and *LVL.* 54 it is mentioned that there were five. There is no *Har.* version extant at the point corresponding to *Egert.* 14.

188–90. Cf. *Egert.* 4, '. . . latrones . . . eius cellam fregerunt et pauperum alimenta, videlicet panem, caseum, cum hiis similibus, rapuerunt. . . .'

191–2. Interpret: 'Thus the Devil led those five villains into temptation in order to cause him to fall (*or* stray) from his chosen way of life.'

193. Cf. 377.

197–9. Cf. Matthew x. 23.

200 ff. *Har.* 5 (p. 130) adds that Robert told his troubles to Helena who consented to his departure and continued to supply his needs in his new home.

201. *Spofford towne.* Modern Spofforth, five miles south-south-east of Knaresborough.

202–5. Cf. *Egert.* 4, '. . . in oracionibus et aliis affliccionibus vacans prolixius persistebat.' This is not included in *Har.*, unless one allows § 5 (p. 130), *Deo vacare desideraret*, when Robert is asking the lady's permission to go to Spofforth.

213–14. Cf. *Egert.* 5, 'Audito enim de Roberti recessu, invitatus est et rogatus a monachis de Hedlay ut cum eis remaneret', which suggests that Robert had, in fact, returned *whar þat hys wounyng was*, i.e. St. Hild's Chapel, and that it was during the stay there that he received the invitation from the monks. In *M.*, although he intends to return to his former dwelling, there is no mention of his having done so; instead he goes to Hedley, apparently on his own initiative.

Har. 5 (p. 130) states that Robert remained at Spofforth for six months, and attributes part of the reason for his departure to the fear of temptation from women.

215. According to *Egert.* 5 and *Har.* 5 (p. 131) the monks invited Robert to live with them when they heard of his departure from Spofforth.

216. *Hedlay*. *Har.* 5 (p. 131) mentions that Hedley was occupied by monks from Holy Trinity, York (*monachi de monasterio Sancte Trinitatis Eboracensis civitatis apud Hedlay commorantes*), who were English Black Monks (D. Knowles, op. cit., p. 67). Hedley was founded in the early twelfth century (T. Tanner, op. cit., p. 650) and dedicated to St. Mary (W. Dugdale, op. cit., iv. 686). According to Canon Solloway (op. cit., p. 68) the site was where now stands Headley Hall, which was partly constructed from the ruins. The name 'Chantry Lane' still survives in the neighbourhood. The district around Bramham Wood and Oglethorpe Hill belonged to the monks (J. Solloway, op. cit., p. 63).

222. *coule*. All the Latin accounts (*Egert.* 5, *Har.* 5 [p. 131], *LVL.* 25) say that Robert had only one garment and do not mention the monks giving him another. Since these were English Black Monks (D. Knowles, op. cit., p. 67) they would not be likely to give him a habit of a white colour as *M.* asserts; he probably acquired it at the Cistercian monastery of Newminster which he visited earlier.

226. At this point in *Egert.* 5 and *Har.* 5 (pp. 131–2) mention is made of the food, which is in *M.* transferred to 273 ff., and there is also in *Egert.* the apostrophe to *myghty men* found in *M.* 285 ff.

227. Cf. Matthew v. 16. The parallel passage occurs at a later point in *Egert.*, in § 9.

233–4. From *Har.* 6 Robert appears to have decided to leave on his own account, and not to have been turned out.

235. *irke*. The meanings given in *OED.* are 'weary, tired, troubled, bored, disgusted, loath', but in the context something stronger is required, such as 'angry', though 'disgusted' might fit.

239. *repentt*. The usual meaning when the verb is intransitive, which might possibly be admitted here, is 'to feel contrition or compunction for something done (usually something that one has done oneself)', but in the context the rarer meaning 'to be sad, mourn (for some happening)' is preferable.

241–4. Cf. *Egert.* 5 and *Har.* 6. The thieves are not mentioned in *Egert.*, but in their stead appears the phrase *in furoribus*. Since there is some similarity in form between *furibus* and *furoribus*, a scribal error may account for this difference.

251-5. Cf. *Har.* 6 and *Egert.* 6. The *mansiounes for hys men*, not mentioned in *Egert.*, seem to be indicated in *Har.*, *habitaculum . . . reciperentur*. In *Har.*, however, Robert himself appears to have carried out the building, though *nobili matrona manum porrigente adiutricem* may refer, without doing so explicitly, to the builders whom the lady sent. *Egert.* mentions them particularly.

In *Har.* 6 more gifts are given to the saint by the lady, and other neighbours also proffer their assistance.

262-4. Cf. *Egert.* 6, 'Sompnum ad mensuram capiens, se prostravit pavimento.' Nothing in *Har.* corresponds to this.

263. *dremyng.* The word may be a verbal noun or the present participle. It is difficult to make sense if it is considered as a noun, and even if taken as a participle the meaning is forced. Interpret: 'A little time that he spent dreaming'; if *droghe* does mean 'spent' it has been influenced by 'dree', OE. *drēogan.*

265-6. As it stands, the passage means 'He hired and had them by him . . . namely four servants', but if *paime* is altered to *panne*, which is a possible alteration, slightly better sense is obtained, 'He hired and had by him then . . . four servants.'

274. *fourth partte.* The meaning is that Robert's bread comprised four-fifths barley-meal and one-fifth ashes (cf. *Egert.* 5, 'Panis vero . . . conficiebatur').

275. *fyfht.* The spelling may be through scribal metathesis of *th*.

277. *potage.* A dish composed of vegetables (*cale* and *leke* and *other herbes*), meat being sometimes included, but not for St. Robert in whose *dysshe was na delytte*. It was boiled in water till soft and appropriately seasoned (*sothen wyth saltte*).

281-2. Despite this statement that he does not know whether Robert ate any kind of flesh, the Latin accounts tell how he refused to eat flesh (*Egert.* 5, *Har.* 5 [pp. 131-2]). Cf. Introduction, p. 28.

283-4. A parallel statement is not found at the corresponding point in *Egert.* or *Har.*, but Robert's drink is mentioned in *Egert.* 14 (*Har.* is not extant at the place which would correspond), though only water is named: *potus, aqua.* The *M.* addition may have been inserted simply to finish the line and thin ale may have seemed quite as unattractive as water to the writer.

297 ff. The omission of the incident of Robert's mother from *Har.* may have been because the author felt that to sacrifice the reputation of the saint's mother would not counterbalance the inclusion of another example of Robert's great powers. Cf. Introduction, p. 31.

300. *hys moder patt was ded.* Gent (op. cit., p. 262) gives an elaborate account of her last illness and death, but most probably this is more a product of his imagination than actual fact. According to him she was buried in Holy Trinity, Micklegate, York, but there is no means

of verifying this. He mentions other members of the family—Walter, who was also buried there, and Jasper, who was buried in the Minster in 1453, but, according to James Torre's manuscript on York Minster (p. 271a) this was a James Flouer, buried in 1452. The same manuscript also mentions John Floure who was buried there in 1502 (see p. 1491a), and, in the index, Robert Flour, a chantry priest, but the page indicated is missing. (These notes on the Torre manuscript have been supplied by Chancellor Harrison of York Minster.)

321. *in the endynge of þat 3ere. Egert.* 7 suggests that it was a full year afterwards that his mother appeared again.

330. *William Scutivyle.* In the heading to this section the form *Stutivilla* is found, and in other books, such as the edited volumes of State Papers, it is a form with *St* that occurs. This is the only occasion on which it is written with a *t* in *M.*, though it would be easy for a scribe to miscopy *t* as *c*. *Egert.* also has forms with *c* but *Har.*, on the one occasion on which the name occurs in the text, reads *t*.

William de Stuteville was Constable of the Castle of Knaresborough. He was still alive on 7 July 1202, when his name appears as a witness to a charter of that date (*Rot. Lit. Pat.*, *4 John*, m. 13, p. 14); a charter of 22 May 1203 (*Rot. Lib.*, *5 John*, m. 13, p. 36) suggests that he was dead, since his share of some land which he and his brother owned was given to the brother. He was, however, certainly dead by 4 June 1203, when the custody of the property he owned *die qua obiit* is given to the Archbishop of Canterbury (*Rot. Lit. Pat.*, *5 John*, m. 10, p. 30). According to *Chron. Lan.*, p. 26, he was buried at Fountains Abbey (*et in capitulo apud Funteyns sepulto*).

337–40. Cf. *Egert.* 8, 'Cui famuli . . . ibidem habitabat' and *Har.* 7, '. . . et nonnullis . . . cognovisset . . .'. The resemblance between *Egert.* and *M.* is much stronger than between them and *Har.*

342. Cf. *Har.* 7, '. . . illumque simulatorem . . . appellans . . . .' *Egert.* does not use 'hypocrite' as one of the epithets William applies to Robert at this point, but he uses it later on in his speech.

342–6. The happiest way of interpreting 344 is to take it with 343 as otherwise one is not told of whom Robert was a *felaghe and a fere*; but 346 requires something to balance it for which *and* is the connecting link, and 344 is the only possibility. Thus some stop must follow *fere*, but as the line does not read quite satisfactorily probably *felaghe and a fere* was included for the alliterative quality rather than for the sense. The only way in which the stop could be made to follow 344 would be to interpret *and* 346 as *also*, thus, 'And said, "This is a hypocrite, abettor, friend, and companion of all the thieves who live here; Robert is also a receiver of all my wild animals that are here."'

Notes

As Miss R. M. Clay (op. cit., pp. 41–42) points out, this accusation was probably not unfounded, though not in the sense that William meant, for Robert, one would imagine, would be a friend to all, rich and poor, honest and dishonest.

347. *By the eghe of God.* This oath is recorded in two of the Latin accounts, *Egert.* 8 and 10 and *Har.* 7, but there, and elsewhere in *M.*, it is always the plural 'eyes'. It is to be noted that William never uses it again after his nightmare.

349. *I sall gar bryn yowe* . . . . It is Robert who is to be burnt and not the servants in *Egert.* 8 and *Har.* 7.

350. *He⟨r⟩ sall he* . . . . This is the better emendation, but *Ne sall he* . . ., 'Nor shall he live (here) longer' is also possible.

355. *aftyr þis. aftyr* can be regarded as either a preposition, 'after this it happened that . . .', or an adverb, 'afterwards this happened, that . . .'.

364. *he sulde gar crake pair croune.* In *Egert.* 8 and *Har.* 7 William threatens to put out his servants' eyes instead. Perhaps the English author preferred an alliterative phrase which came readily to his mind and which would have the same force as a threat.

395. *hend.* No satisfactory meaning has been found for this word. A development of OE. *hīgna, hīna* (g.pl. of *hīgan*), meaning 'hind, servant', is unlikely as *OED.* suggests that *d* forms do not appear till the sixteenth century, and, in addition, the vowel would be peculiar. The following suggestions may be made, but none is adequate. (1) A Nthn. pl. of *hand* from ON. *hend,* but then it would have to be assumed that *a* meant 'all': *of a hend* would mean 'from all sides'. (2) Connected in some way with OE. *gehende,* 'near at hand'. (3) A rare form of *end,* and *of a hend* might mean 'from a remote place'. Unfortunately none of the Latin accounts affords any help with this phrase, which is probably only a tag.

403. The heading above this line cannot be translated as it stands in the manuscript; *vapare* is no doubt a mistake for *vaporem.*

405. *Outt of the North Countre.* Again the direction is different in *Egert.* 10 where it is *de australi parte.* Either direction could be correct as no indication is given as to what William had been doing immediately previous to this time, but if the author were a Northerner, then he would prefer northern geography. Cf. the notes to 99 and 836.

431. In the heading above this line the letters between *tres* and *erunt* are very indistinct. The letter preceding *erunt* is possibly an *i* as there seems to be a faint trace of a stroke above. Preceding that is the contraction for either *er/ir* or *re* (only the top of the loop is visible so one cannot be sure which it is), and preceding that there may be two letters or only one. The reconstruction to *viri,* which would give sense, could be made, but it is by no means certainly right. *Willelm* lacks its inflexional ending, most probably *o.*

433. *moysand in mynd.* 'In a comatose condition', no doubt induced by the wine.

434. *blakker pan ynd. ynd* may be interpreted as 'India' or 'indigo', but the latter is preferable. *Egert.* 10 has *fuligine nigriores.*

435. *trayle.* In *Egert.* 10 the *trayle* is flaming with fire—*traham ferream igne flammantem*—and with this the sleeper's sides are struck.

459–72. Cf. *Egert.* 10, 'Tunc Wyllelmus mero motu . . . penuria pregravatis.'

460. *Grymbalde Kyrkstane.* Drake (op. cit., p. 373) says that the boundary was *Grimbald-cragg-stone*, and Hargrove (op. cit., p. 7) *Grimbald-bridge*, both of which are given by Gent (op. cit., p. 265). No other mention of the *Kyrkstane* has been found, apart from *Egert.* 10, but Grimbald Bridge spans the Nidd near St. Robert's Cave on the Knaresborough–Wetherby road, and Grimbald Crag is on the Nidd a little below Knaresborough.

463 ff. In *Chron. Lan.* (p. 26) William grants Robert two cows and two horses annually, and also additional gifts: *domum pro pauperibus suscipiendis, et horreum pro reponendis* (but compare these with the widow's gifts, *M.* 251–5).

468–9. *Fray Yole Day . . . folowand.* That is, from Christmas Day to the day after Epiphany; the latter is stated definitely in *Egert.* 10.

485. *Walter.* Though Walter, like his father, is usually described as 'mayor of York', it is not certain that even in his time the modern meaning can be applied. (Cf. the note to 49.)

494. *dyd.* Interpret: 'has done'.

507. *Hym.* From the sense this must refer to Robert, but from the construction it could be equally well a reference to Walter.

508. *Egert.* 11 explains further that the establishment was enlarged for the reception of poor people and pilgrims journeying to Jerusalem, and that the devil attempted to uproot the buildings and get rid of the people.

516. *Yue.* Drake (op. cit., pp. 373–4) would seem to have misread this name, calling him 'Jew' throughout his account. In the note on this name in *The Oxford Dictionary of English Christian Names* (Oxford, 1946) E. G. Withycombe derives *Yue* from OF. *Ives, Ivon*, which probably had an earlier Celtic origin. It is also pointed out that the name was a popular one among the Anglo-Normans. Another bearer of the name was the legendary saint after whom the town of St. Ives in Huntingdonshire was called.

528. *helpe.* This form appears to be 3 sg. pa. and can be accounted for if the preterite has gone over into the weak verbs and then lost the final *d*, either in current speech or by scribal error. It is less likely that the form is a strong pa. sg. as it would then be the only form in the text in which *e* is found for OE. *a* before *l* | consonant.

530. A long homily is delivered to Yve at this point in *Egert.* 12.

552. *M.* omits the rather amusing passage in *Egert.* 13 about Yve's annoyance when Robert smiles at him in his plight, '*Ubi est,*' *ait Yvo,* '*hic sermo . . . cum flentibus?*'

561. *he.* The pronoun could refer equally well to Robert or Yve, but *Egert.* 14 shows that Yve is the person meant.

569. *gryme.* In *OED.* 'grim' v. means, in the transitive sense, 'to make grim or fierce, cause to look grim &c.', with late quotations; 'grime' v. may mean 'to befoul, blacken, cover with grime' which is slightly better for the context if used figuratively, though not very good. A word such as 'punish' would suit best.

570. *Yff ytt be taryed, ytt.* . . . This line will make sense as it stands, but would make better if the second *ytt* were emended to *3ytt.*

576. *Erll.* Presumably William de Stuteville is meant.

586. *arest hyr in a band.* In *Egert.* 15 Robert captures the cow by throwing his arms round her neck.

591 ff. This story was recorded in a stained-glass window of Knaresborough Parish Church, made in 1473, and the glass was there in 1622 (see Roger Dodsworth, *Yorkshire Church Notes 1619-31,* ed. J. W. Clay [Yorkshire Archaeological Society, 1904], Record Series, xxxiv, 158), but it has since been removed.

593 ff. Cf. the Knaresborough saying 'As freely at (*sic*) St. Robert gave his cow', cited in *The White Rose Garland* (ed. W. J. Halliday and A. S. Umpleby [London, 1949]), p. 142, No. 210.

593-4. For the rhyme between these two lines see Introduction, p. 13 and note 2.

613. *skorne.* The meaning in the context is not clear, but interpret *þou schapes þi skorne* as 'You are contriving what will cause your scorn'. This may be an attempt to render the Latin, *Sed tibi continget quod fingere presumpsisti (Egert.* 15).

614. *haue.* This translates the future tense of *habebit (Egert.* 15).

631 ff. This story was also recorded in a church window. The glass was originally at Dale Abbey in Derbyshire, but was later removed to Morley Church, in the same county, where it is still to be seen. The story depicted in the window differs from the version given here principally in that Robert's dealings about the stags are with the king.

675. *wype.* The bird has a reputation for being angry when roused. Cf. 'Parlyament of Byrdes' in *Harleian Miscellany* (London, 1810), v, p. 510: *Though thou be hasty as the Wype.*

681. At this point in *Egert.* 17 the devil finds Robert sleeping after his night of prayer and taunts him.

698. There is no mention of the devil's having left any trace. At this point in *Egert.* 18 he leaves a stench, and, corresponding to 723 ff., filthy tracks (*Egert.* 19).

Gerrard. See the note by Professor Bruce Dickins on Gerrard as a goblin-name in *T.L.S.* for 1941, p. 55.

702. *Off seuen ʒeres. Egert.* 19 reads *duodecim.*

703. The omission of the subject in the sentence requires the inclusion of 'he' in the interpretation.

715–17. Cf. *Egert.* 19, 'Alio quoque tempore, Sathanas in specie pueri sexdecim annorum se transformavit.'

723. The subject in this line is the devil, whereas in the preceding lines it has been Robert. The change in subject is not certain until 726, the fourth line of the devil's speech.

726. *rusty.* The sense 'morally foul or corrupt' need not be emphasized here as the word is used merely as a general term of opprobrium.

736. *fytte.* Two distinct meanings are found in ME. for the word— (1) from OE. *fitt,* strong fem., 'part or section of a poem or song; a canto', and (2) from OE. *fitt* of uncertain gender which occurs only once, 'conflict, struggle; painful or exciting experience', and from this has developed Mod.E. *fit* (epileptic). If the first OE. word is the source of *fytte,* then the meaning must be somewhat looser to suit the context and must refer to the matter which forms the 'part' or 'section', namely the 'incident', unless *of a* can be interpreted 'in a'. If, however, it is to be derived from (2) then interpret 'an exciting event'.

737–9. 739 shows that a stop must come at the end of 738. The phrase *Hys celle to se* will fit in equally well with the line that precedes and the phrase that follows it. If the former interpretation is admitted, then *he him besoght* must be parenthetic, but if the latter, the two lines can be read without forcing the meaning.

737. *Bryane.* Brian de L'Isle or de Insula. Only *Chron. Lan.* among the Latin accounts of Robert mentions the succession of Brian to the office of Constable of Knaresborough Castle: *Briano de Insula, a rege Johanne totum illius patriae dominium collatum est* (p. 26). Brian supported John in his struggle against the Barons, and is mentioned by Matthew Paris among the king's evil counsellors (*Chronica Majora,* ed. H. R. Luard [London, 1874], ii. 533). After John's death Brian pursued the system of rapine and plunder that he had followed under that king (*Chronica Majora, ut sup.* [London, 1876], iii. 33), but eventually he submitted to Henry III (ibid., p. 83), and afterwards was given official duties by him, as is shown by the many references to him in the edited volumes of State Papers.

King John visited Knaresborough several times between February 1206 and February 1216 ('Itinerary of King John' in *Rot. Lit. Pat.*), but Brian apparently did not take him to meet Robert until 1216, as the grant to the saint of half a carucate of land *in Boscho de Swenesco* is dated 24 February 1216 (*Rot. Lit. Claus., 17 John,* m. 10 [i. 249]).

761. '*Sir,*' *he sayd* .... Though no indication is given, presumably Brian is about to speak in Robert's defence, since he is his friend, but his contribution to the conversation has not been sufficiently

Notes

recent for him to be referred to simply as *he*. Corresponding to *he sayd*, Egert. 20 reads *responderunt*.

771. *Tha⟨n⟩*. It is best to assume that a contraction mark for *n* has been omitted over the *a*. A less likely possibility is that the manuscript reading is a scribal error for *Yha*.

775 ff. Yve appears to have more of a head for business than Robert and does not like to lose a good opportunity.

806. *housebandry*. The sense of the word which fits here is 'the cultivation of the soil', and the line may be then rendered 'about the cultivation of the soil by means of his plough'.

807 ff. According to *Chron. Lan.*, p. 27, the *persone* went to see Robert at the instigation of Alexander Dorset, *quidam jurisperitus*.

818. The meaning of the line seems to be 'never before till now has it produced a crop (an increase)'. *newed* is used of the yearly increase of produce, but *OED.* affords no definite help with this word, or with the meaning of *cresse*.

820. *forthi*. This appears in the manuscript as *for thi*; it is unlikely that this should be interpreted as 'for yourself', so to read *forthi*, meaning 'therefore', is to be preferred.

836. *Into this North* . . . . *Egert.* 22 reads *ad australes partes*. As with 405 and the parallel *Egert.* passage, either direction could be correct as, according to the edited volumes of State Papers, Brian appears to have had business in both the North and the South, and nothing indicates the specific expedition to which reference is being made here; but, again, if the author of *M.* was a Northerner, then he preferred northern geography. The fact that the demonstrative adjective *this* is used and not *the* might be considered to show that the writer lived farther north if Brian set out on the journey from Knaresborough. See Introduction, pp. 26–27.

854. *pair he dyed*. This statement is misleading. One would assume from it that Brian died not very long after this date, which must have been before Robert's death in 1218. But Brian's name is mentioned many times after this date, usually in his office as Justice of the Forest (it may have been in this capacity that he was journeying north, since the office entailed visitation). He was without doubt dead by 6 September 1234 (*Close Rolls, 18 Hen. III*, m. 8 [*1231–4*, p. 512]), but he probably died in August 1234, for on the 15th it is granted that 'at whatever time before his death he may choose to make his will, he shall have free disposition of making his will of his movables . . .' (*Pat. Rolls, 18 Hen. III*, m. 7 [*1232–47*, p. 64]), and on 18 August the King is taking into his own hands *terras quae fuerunt Briani de Insula* (*Rot. Fin., 18 Hen. III*, m. 4 [i. 263]).

866. *Fountaunce*. The monks of Fountains would know much of Robert's fame since their abbey is not far from Knaresborough.

877–904. This is an expansion on the part of the author of *M.* or his immediate source(s), but in a manner similar to passages in *Egert.* which are usually abbreviated in *M.*

899. *romaunce.* The word is used with reference to the language in which the work is written, and usually this indicates the vernacular language of French as opposed to Latin. The source which the ME. author used may have been an Anglo-French work which has since disappeared; if there were such a source it might correspond to *Y,* which, according to the Introduction, p. 32, was the source of *M.* On the other hand it is just possible that the author is using the word with a different application and is referring to a Latin source, which may have been not unlike *Egert.*; then *romaunce* would imply an extended usage here, and would refer to a language other than the writer's own vernacular.

899–900. Although the *l* has been retained in the spelling of *werlde,* yet the rhyme with *herd* suggests that it was no longer pronounced. Cf. the rhymes 477–8, 927–8, 1083–4.

907–10. These lines are difficult to interpret, though the general sense is clear, viz. death carries off everyone whatever his condition, worldly, physical, or moral. One interpretation is 'through death which spares neither duke nor king nor sovereign; nothing can save sinful or saint, rich or poor, or make anyone well or ill'. Here the difficulty lies in *sound ne sore,* for the point is that nothing saves anyone from death, and the effects of death, whether for good or ill, are not under consideration, as death is regarded as sufficient evil in itself. To avoid this difficulty the last piece could be interpreted 'nothing can make safe sinful or saint, rich or poor, healthy or ill'. In both cases, if *sore* is taken to mean 'ill', derived from OE. *sār,* it is to be noted that on every other occasion in the text the word has the vowel *a,* and also that if *sayff* is considered in the first interpretation as an infinitive, in the definite verbal forms in the text the form is always *sau-.*

918. *blesse.* In this form from OE. *bliss* the *e* is probably a scribal error as the rhyme with *wyshe* (OE. *wissian*) shows that *i* is required. Cf. also *Provenance,* A. 5. (Introduction, p. 11.)

932. *habytt whytt.* The habit of the Cistercian Order.

939. Although the monks succeeded in clothing Robert's body in their habit (cf. *Egert.* 24, *eum habitu suo induerunt*), yet the people of Knaresborough prevented them from carrying it off with them to Fountains (cf. *M.* 951 ff. and *Egert.* 24).

943. *He . . . sweltt.* The date of Robert's death is given in *Chron. Lan.,* p. 25, as 24 September (*octavo kalendas Octobris*) 1218, but in the *Dictionary of National Biography,* xlviii. 361 as 1235(?). This latter date cannot be right, since the grant was made to Yve in 1227 of all the lands which Robert had owned, and Robert is described as

Notes

'formerly hermit there' (*Char. Rolls, 12 Hen. III*, m. 10 [*1226-57*, p. 66]).

946. *hys.* This may be the possessive pronoun used absolutely (interpret: 'Honoured it as being one of His [chosen ones]'), or it may be the form equivalent in sense to ME. *hem, paim* (interpret: 'Honoured it as being one of themselves').

953. The ostensible reason for carrying away the body—described with more detail in *Egert.* 24—was that the consecrated grounds of the monastery were a more fitting resting-place for the saint than the Chapel of the Holy Rood, but in reality the monks knew that whosoever possessed the body possessed also a potential source of income which could be derived from the pilgrims to the tomb. The body is no longer in the Chapel of the Holy Rood, and it seems that it was taken to the Trinitarian House at Knaresborough, according to a Papal Letter which speaks of the 'monastery of St. Robert of Gnarebur . . . where that saint's body is buried' (*Papal Letters*, i. 277). The gravestone of Sir Henry Slingsby in Knaresborough Parish Church bears an inscription to the effect that it once covered Robert's tomb, but the shape is completely different from that of the tomb in the Chapel of the Holy Rood. However, the inscription perhaps lends support to the suggestion that the body was removed to the Priory, since the stone may have been taken from the later resting-place.

954-5. *Bott Knaresburgh . . . araed routte.* There are three possible meanings here : (1) Knaresborough knew about them, equipped a company of men-at-arms. (2) Knaresborough knew about them, (sent) a fully equipped company. . . . (3) Knaresborough knew about them ; a fully equipped company . . . (went). In every case by *Knaresborough* must be understood 'the people of Knaresborough'.

969. Cf. Introduction, p. 5. *Egerton* 22.

971 ff. Matthew Paris mentions the cures that were effected at Robert's grave, e.g. *Chronica Majora*, ed. H. R. Luard (London, 1876), iii. 521: 1238. *De fama sancti Roberti Heremitae de Cnareburc. Eodemque anno claruit fama sancti Roberti heremitae apud Knareburc, cujus tumba oleum medicinale fertur abundanter emisisse.* J. R. Walbran (op. cit., p. 170 n.) prosaically attributes this oil to 'the solution of the resinous substance with which the cover may have been fixed'.

Chronica Majora, ut sup. (London, 1877), iv. 378: 1244. Miracles at various tombs in England, . . . *sicut ad tumbam beati Roberti de Karreburg, choruscare, et sanitatum beneficia aegrotis ad laudem Christi fuisse distributa.*

977. *menbirs.* There is an OF. *menbre* as well as *membre*, from which *menbirs* may be derived, but it is more probable that the accidental omission of a minim accounts for the form in the text.

990. *patrone.* This may be used in the technical religious sense, 'the founder of a religious order', cf. *The English Works of Wyclif*, ed. F. D. Matthew (E.E.T.S. 1880), p. 285: *Also crist & his apostlis techen vs to lyue beter þanne þes patrouns of þes newe ordris*. In that case the author must have held the belief, not infrequent at one time, though there is no proof for the assumption, that St. Robert established the Order of Trinitarians in England. However, the word was not uncommonly used in a more general sense, so this would not necessarily follow.

995. A verb needs to be included here in the interpretation: 'All prayers are thus for their house.'

1022. *Couerham*. An abbey in the North Riding of Yorkshire. See *V.C.H., Yorks*. iii. 243–5.

1031–2. The probable interpretation is 'and thus the Order of the Holy Trinity took it over and remained there always (*ay to be*)', though *sway* could be interpreted as 'while it was in this condition', i.e. deserted.

1035. From this point to 1128 it is possible to trace some resemblance between *D*. and *HT*. With 1035–7 cf. *HT*. 15.

1038. Cf. *HT*. 24 in which the second division of the goods is to be given to *servos ... de coquina*.

1039–54. Cf. *HT*. 16–23 which mentions rather more ways in which the captives 'beyond the seas' are afflicted.

1045–6. The rhyme is assonantal, rather than perfect, unless *Sara-ȝyns* should show a full inflexional ending *-is*, which would then form the rhyme.

1055–64. Cf. *HT*. 28–30, where the scriptures are also quoted in support of the argument that although he is in charge of a house, yet a minister is still expected to be as a servant. The interpretation of 1055–8 is difficult. The meaning may be 'Thus you may interpret *mynistre*, by saying that he is only a servant, even if he yet occupies his position in the way that a prelate ought to do', i.e. even if he is surrounded by all the trappings and honours usual for a cleric of high rank. Another interpretation is 'Thus you may . . . servant; (but) even if he serves, yet his rank is (as high) as (that of) a prelate ought to be.'

1055. *Mynistre*. *Minister* is the Latin title given to the brother in charge of a Trinitarian house: *Fratres domus Ordinis Sanctae Trinitatis, et Captivorum, sub obedientia Praelati domus suae, qui Minister vocabitur, in castitate & sine proprio vivant*. (Laertii Cherubini *Magnum Bullarium Romanum* [Rome, 1638], i. 145.)

1060. This is again a difficult line, which probably means 'which may be agreeable to this priest' or 'to which this priest may agree'.

1065–72. Cf. *HT*. 11–14. Cf. also the explanation of the colours given by Deslandres (op. cit., p. 26): '*Le blanc*, couleur parfaite,

Notes

figurant le Père; le *bleu*, le Fils, à cause des souffrances de la Passion, et le *rouge*, le Saint-Esprit.'

1073–7. Cf. *HT*. 5–10, where the subject is expounded at greater length.

1078–98. Cf. *HT*. 31–34. *HT*. says that the hermits went to the Pope *pro securitate vite* (33).

1099–1112. Cf. *HT*. 35–38. Whereas in *D*. it is an angel who appears with the habit, it is God Himself in *HT*.

1113–24. Cf. *HT*. 39–42.

1125–8. Cf. *HT*. 43–44, which is more detailed.

1128. For other and different accounts of the foundation of the Trinitarian Order see Deslandres (op. cit., ii, *Pièces justificatives*). The prose account is from Bibl. Nat., ms. lat. 9753, f⁰ 10v⁰, and the verse account from Bibl. Nat., ms. lat. 9753, f⁰ 12v⁰.

1129. *confessour*. A technical term used of one who avows his religion in the face of danger, but who does not suffer martyrdom. At an early date, however, the term would appear to have been used in a somewhat wider sense, as is suggested by the early ascription of the title to Edward the Confessor. In the Preface to the *Book of Saints* (*ut sup*.), p. x, it is explained that 'liturgically, Saints are classified as Apostles, Martyrs, Bishops or Confessors', and the last group includes those saints who cannot be classified under the other three headings.

1143. *fuffylled*. The manuscript reading may be a scribal error for *fulfylled*, but, on the other hand, *ff* may show assimilation of *lf*.

1154. Interpret: 'Therefore my life cannot be lightened (of its load of sin).'

1168–72. Interpret: 'I beseech you to send us, who dwell in this place, grace, strength and power to serve you without sin, and so that with our service we may always completely please you here.' It is better to take the clause *þat we maye* . . . as dependent on *send vs grace*. &c., rather than on *besek*.

1173. *helpe*. A verb, either an infinitive co-ordinate with *send*, 'I beseech you to help us . . .' or a pr. sub. co-ordinate with *besek*, 'And do you help us . . . .'

1177. *dedlye synnes*. The theme of the Seven Deadly Sins was treated very frequently in medieval literature; Chaucer's *Parson's Tale* deals at length with the subject. The Sins were divided into sins of the flesh and sins of the spirit, Superbia being reckoned as the worst. In the present text, 1191–1208, the requests made may be with reference to protection from the Sins, viz. Superbia 1192–3, 1199–1200; Accidia 1194; Ira 1197–8, 1205, 1207–8; Luxuria 1201; Gula 1203; Invidia 1195–6, 1202, 1204. Avaritia may also be included since the descriptions of some of the Sins are not very definite.

1179–90. These lines show a confused construction which can be interpreted best if 1185-8 (perhaps 1184 also, though this line will fit in with 1183 equally well) are assumed to be parenthetic, thus: 'And of your kindness grant me grace thus to govern this house justly, and thus to rule as befits my position that I, even if I am humble, occupy as president through the favour which God has sent to me here—may it be for the salvation of this community and for the good fortune and healthy maintaining of the house on account of my control.' *helpe* (1189) seems to balance *sauyng* and *mede* (1190), and must therefore be a noun; the only verb expressed on which these could depend is *graunt* (1179).

1191 ff. A confused construction is again to be noticed here. 1192-4 depend on *beseke* (1191); 1195-6 are almost parenthetic as they introduce a fresh construction; 1197 ff. depend on *I the beseke ... to be ...* (1191-2).

1213-14. If some infinitive meaning 'to obtain' may be understood before these lines, then they can depend on *gar me* (1210).

1218. *seryne or shwed*. No vowel is shown in the stem of *shwed*, but, since it rhymes with *lewed*, it is reasonable to suppose that the word is from OE. *scēawian*. Cf. the rhymes 889-90.

seryne. As it stands this word makes no sense. Some contrast is obviously required between *seryne* and *shwed* to balance *lered* and *lewed* of the previous line, and the meaning seems to be 'enclosed', i.e. those nuns who never came out into the world again after taking their vows, as opposed to those who were *shwed*, i.e. allowed to mingle with the laity when necessary. It is possible that the scribe misread a *c* as an *e*, and then the original would be *scryne*. There may be some connexion between this and the verb 'to shrine', derived from OE. *scrīn*, and one of the meanings given for this in *OED*. is 'to dwell as in a shrine'. It must be pointed out that the pa. p., the form to be expected in the phrase, has a final *d* in every quotation in *OED*. However, there are four occasions in this text on which a final *d* seems to have been omitted, *helpe* 528, *spekan* 845, *an* 295, 1290.

1219. This line may be taken with 1218 or 1220.

1229-31. Though the construction in these lines seems the same, yet the sense shows that a pause must follow 1230 as the first two lines are dependent on *lele louyng be* 1226, and the last must be taken with 1232: 'Send (1224) help, well-being and a holy way of life to my companions every one.'

1246. *Tha⟨t⟩*. The manuscript reading *Tha* may be a mistake for either *Than* or *That*, but of the two the latter gives rather the better sense.

1273. Lines 1274-1305 are all dependent on this line.

1275-6. *dremes*. This is the only obvious example of an inflexional ending alone forming the rhyme. Cf. 1045-6.

1292. Interpret: '(Keep me) from being afflicted with distress.'

SELECT GLOSSARY

k and *c* are treated together under *c*, and *i* and *y* under *i*; *u* and *v* appear as *v* initially and generally as *u* medially.

n following a number indicates a reference to the *Notes*.

Unimportant differences in spelling have not been recorded, e.g. *i* for *y*, the appearance or non-appearance of final *e*.

A

a *adv.* quite 1112.
abaste *v.* confounded 720.
abyde *v.* endure 534, 888; ~**and** persevering 118.
abstinentt *adj.* sparing, frugal 1203.
accorde *v.* agree, consent 1060.
ake *n.* oak tree 742.
aghen *adj.* own 936, 1129; *n.* own goods 829.
ay *indef. art.* a 208.
ayled *v.* ailed 972.
ayther *pron.* each of two 104, 490, 1087.
alde *adj.* old 612, 857.
all *conj.* although; ~ **yff** even if 1057, 1182.
almose *n.* alms, charitable relief 176, 269, 563, &c.
als *adv.* as 9, 28, 266, &c.; as, while 333, 407, 433, &c.; also 893, 1213.
althir *adv.* of all; ~ **nexte** next of all, thereupon 328.
amend *v.* divert 160; make amends, alter 456.
amese *v.* alleviate 1195.
anely *prep.* except 1086.
anes *adv.* once 573.
appropird *v.* set aside 817.
approued *v.* proved, shown 18.
appurtinaunce *n.* belongings, appendages 1019.
araed *v.* arrayed, equipped 955 n.
arest *v.* seize, capture 155; seized, captured 586.
as *n.* ashes 275; **asse** 1138.
assentt *v.* agreed 649.
athe *n.* oath 425.
avised *v.* counselled 862.
avowe *n.* patron saint 1174.
awe *v.* ought 1058.

awter *n.* altar 967.

B

baile *n.* misery, unhappiness 295, 304, 380, &c.; **bales** 536.
bane *n.* bone, leg 625; **bayn** 543; **blode and** ~ wholly 326.
banned *v.* cursed 361.
baran *adj.* barren 983.
barefotte *adj.* barefoot 562.
barne *n.* child 52, 323.
bedeyn *adv.* immediately 647.
bedes *n.* prayers 1005.
begyled *v.* foiled 568.
beyn *v.* been 141, 218.
beld *v.* dwell 243, 1315; ~**es** 492; ~**ed** 336; **beilde** assist, help 513.
belyue *adv.* quickly 549; ~**lyffe** 983.
belle *n.* fire, blaze 349.
bemeynes *v.* means, signifies 412.
bere *n.* bier 963.
besand *n.* bezant (coin) 1118.
besily *adv.* earnestly 748.
besines *n.* business, task, occupation 513.
byddynges *n.* commands 352.
bygge *v.* build 252, 507; ~**d** 336, 387.
byggynges *n.* establishment, buildings 348, 353, 359, 363.
byll *n.* written statement 1089, 1092, 1094.
bysen *adj.* blind, purblind 976.
bytyng *n.* attack 1283.
blaym *n.* blame 418; injury 958.
ble *n.* colour 1101.
blesse *n.* joy, blessedness 918.
blysse *v.* bless 326, 842; ~**d** 375, 556, 844, &c.; **blyste** 953.
bode *v.* behoved; **hym** ~ he must needs 906.
boghe *n.* branch 543.

H

102 Select Glossary

borde n. table, meals 1203.
bost v. threatened 361.
bott adv. only 43, 224, 1056, 1150; conj. ~ **yff** unless 347, 363.
boune adj. ready; **be** ~ make one's way 421; **mayde hym / þaim** ~ made his / their way 91, 382, 961.
bouned v. got ready 430.
bour n. dwelling, hut 188.
bouse v. bow; ~ **to obey** 122; **bowes** happen 554.
boxum adj. obedient 1199.
brathe adj. impetuous, angry 352.
brefed v. written 94.
brere n. briar 436.
brest v. burst 1146.
brether n. brothers in God 1217.
bryn v. burn 349.
busked v. prepared, got ready 430, 549.
buskes n. bushes 387, 492.

C, K

kayred see **caryed**.
cayteyff n. captive, wretch 607; **catyeff** 400; ~**es** 642; **cayteffys** 1053, 1115, 1122; **catyffes** 564.
cald n. cold 226, 1294.
cale n. cabbage 277.
cambe n. comb 475.
carefully adv. full of care 447.
caryed v. went, departed 207, 215, 959; **kayred** 136.
carle n. countryman, servant 693.
carpyng n. story, narration 38, 44.
kastes v. throws up 163; **kest** cast, threw 398, 1102; **cast** reckon, sum up 1310.
catyeff, &c. see **cayteyff**.
caytefte n. wretchedness, misery 1135; **caty**~ 1296.
key n. cows 465.
keyn adj. bold, proud, cruel 429, 1280, 1290.
kemmes v. combs, chastises 475.
kempes n. champions 41.
kenne v. make known, introduce 750.
certes adv. indeed 786.
kerued v. carved 890.
kest see **kastes**.

cetiȝand n. citizen (of heaven) 1155.
chached v. caught, overcome 607, 1115.
chanons n. canons, priests 1024.
chastes v. chastises 474.
chawfed v. grew angry 360.
chere n. mood, disposition, intention 884.
chese v. chose 874.
kyrke n. church 236, 807.
kytte n. belly 163.
clargy n. knowledge, skill 84.
clennes n. cleanness, purity 1072.
cleth v. clothe, dress 1104; **cled** 222, 939, 1110.
clethinge n. garment, clothing 1065, 1068, 1102, &c.
cleues v. is attached 1073.
closter n. cloister, monastery 236, 497.
knytt v. joined 1033.
collacioune n. community, conference 111.
combraunce n. hindrance, trouble 1296.
comly adj. gracious 745.
compacientt adj. sympathetic, understanding 1207.
condigne adj. honourable, worthy 752.
konnyng n. knowledge 26.
consaued v. learnt 78.
cote n. dwelling 413.
couent n. monastery 497.
couettys v. covets 827.
coule n. habit, cloak 222, 224, 939.
counsayll n. counsel, advice 111, 133, 600; council 1095.
countes n. accounts 1310.
couped v. confounded, made to pay dearly 1159.
couth v. knew how to, was able 60, 84, 878, &c.
crake v. crack 364.
crafte n. skill, knowledge, craft 251; ~**s** 506.
crage n. cliff, rock 879.
crased v. infirm, deformed, misshapen 973.
cresse n. crop 818 n.

Select Glossary

creues *n.* small hole, cave 20, 879.
creule *v.* crawl 878.
crysten *adj.* Christian 1042, 1052, 1053.
croked *adj.* deformed, crooked 612, 973.
crossed *v.* made the sign of the Cross over 713.
croune *n.* head, skull 364; crown 745.
crowell *adj.* cruel 475, 1280.
cure *n.* care, cure (of souls) 564, 1228.

D

dayle *n.* vale, world 864.
dayntes *n.* luxuries, choice morsels 287.
daynty *adj.* excellent 1007.
dampnacion *n.* condemnation 1157.
debaytte *n.* dispute 1030.
deboner *adj.* mild, gentle 63.
ded *n.* death 897, 984, 1275, &c.
dede *n.* deed, action; **in hys ~ indeed** 488.
dedlye *adj.* deadly 1177, 1301.
dee *v.* die 941; **deghe** 871, 935; **deghes** 828; **dyed** 854, 1007.
deiff *adj.* deaf 973.
dele *n.* whit, part; **euerylkay ~** without doubt 428.
dele *v.* give away, share out 528, 828; **deltt** 1037; deal with 814.
delyte *n.* joy 110; tastiness, attraction 280.
deme *v.* judge 8.
dere *n.* harm, injury 885, 1002.
dere *v.* harm 803; **~d** annoyed, disturbed 237.
derfely *adv.* fiercely, violently 444.
detbundon *adj.* obliged, honour-bound 1121.
dett *n.* transgression 1177, 1301.
deuyne *v.* guess, think 424.
deuised *v.* divided 1037.
diamaunde *n.* diamond, outstanding person 1139, 1156.
dyed see **dee**.
digne *adj.* noble, worthy 803.

dylle *v.* assuage, soothe 1140.
dyng *v.* raze, knock 348, 427; **dang** 363, 367; **dongen** 381.
dirigees *n.* dirges 950.
discrecion *n.* discrimination 1237.
discryffe *v.* describe 680, 898.
dishese *n.* discomfort, misery 885, 1042, 1140, &c.
distroes *v.* destroy 638; **doune ~** undo, ruin 444.
doynges *n.* doings, deeds 1150.
dole *n.* grief, sorrow 1297.
doluen *v.* buried 871, 1245.
dome *n.* judgement 1160.
domicelle *n.* dwelling 427.
domme *adj.* dumb 973.
dowte *n.* doubt 373.
draffe *v.* drove 654.
drang *v.* drank 283.
dre *v.* endure, live 661; **drye** 1215.
drery *adj.* sorrowful, unhappy 852.
dresse *v.* direct 110, 1157; **~d** 67.
drye see **dre**.
droghe *v.* spent 263 n.
dubbed *v.* filled, adorned 150.
dughty *adj.* fitting, great 1244.
durese *n.* hardship 885.

E

ee see **eghe**.
eft *adv.* again 164.
efter *prep.* according to 26, 31; after 897, 1015; *adv.* afterwards 431.
eftirward *adv.* afterwards 403, 484.
eftsones *adv.* soon 861.
eghe *n.* eye 347, 947; **ee** 704; **~n** 362, 420.
enpeched *v.* accused 230.
enposynnyng *n.* poisoning 1281.
enseging *v.* surrounding, attacking 1298.
ententt *n.* intention, purpose 147, 504; **in~** 1091.
ere *n.* ear of corn 753, 756.
etchewand *v.* avoiding 62; **~ed** 82, 256.
euerylkay *adj.* every 428; **euiralkay** 1199.

F

fay *n.* foe, enemy 258, 546; **faes** 55.
fayland *n.* apostate 166.
fayne *adj.* glad 249, 546.
fair *adj.* noble, gracious, worthy 146.
fair *adv.* graciously 217; **fare** 490.
faythfully *adv.* earnestly 105.
faytour *n.* deceiver, villain, impostor 601, 617; ~**tors** 191.
fanded *v.* tried, led into temptation 192.
fandyng *n.* temptation 156, 376, 733.
far *n.* state, condition 308.
fare *adv.* see **fair**.
fare *v.* go, fare 579; ~**d** 35, 383, 437.
farly see **ferly**.
fatt *adj.* greasy 686.
fautes *n.* faults, sins 312, 1298.
fautour *n.* abettor, patron 343.
fekyll *adj.* treacherous, deceitful 242.
feght *v.* fight 55.
felagh *n.* companion 157, 343; **felaw** 149; ~**es** 242, 1231; **felawes** 79; **felawe sir** 146.
fele *adj.* many 312.
fell *adj.* fierce, ruthless 153, 197, 692, 1279.
fell *v.* fell, cause to fall or stray 192, 733; ~**ed** 57.
fell *v.* happened 431.
fend *n.* the Devil 56, 153, 191, &c.; **feynd** 1161, 1214; devil, fiend 396, 979; ~**ys** 802, 1279.
ferd *v.* went 157.
fere *n.* companion 343.
fere *n.* company; **in** ~ together 559, 985.
fere *adj.* strong, absolute 69.
ferly *n.* marvel 431, 591; **farly** 328; marvels 890.
ferre *adv.* afar off 20.
fersly *adv.* fiercely 442.
fest *n.* feast, banquet 35.
fyfht *num.* fifth 275.
fyld *v.* filled, occupied 66.
fynd *v.* provide, provide for 1023; **fand** 270.
fytte *n.* incident 736 n.
flamme *n.* flame, blaze 714.
flytte *v.* grow abusive 341.
flytte *v.* pass, depart 259, 735, 979.
fode *n.* food 248; creature 194.
fole *n.* fool 760, 783; ~**s** 197.
foly *n.* folly 66, 1161.
fordo *v.* put an end to 1140.
forfett *n.* crime, offence 399.
forged *v.* devised, contrived 537, 601.
forsoth *adv.* indeed, certainly 795.
forthi *conj.* therefore 157, 820, 889, 1001.
forthoght *v.* displeased, annoyed 734.
fotte *n.* foot 555, 617; **fett** feet 454, 633.
found *v.* go, journey 1270.
fourme *v.* fashion, devise 1161.
fray *prep.* from 30, 160, 192, &c.; **fra** 207, 304, 904, &c.
frayned *v.* asked 308.
fre *adj.* noble 1022, 1119, 1174, &c.
freke *n.* creature, warrior, person 437.
freinde *n.* friend, kinsman 258, 522, 838; **frendes** 35, 129; **frende** patron 783.
frely *adv.* graciously, willingly 662.
frenesyse *n.* phrenetics, epileptics 981.
frenshipe *n.* friends 129.
frere *n.* brother, monk 29 n., 101, 105.
fretand *v.* afflicting, mortifying 70, 116.
fryth *n.* game-preserve, wooded country 332.
fulfylled *v.* fulfilled, inspired 72; **fuffylled** 1143 n.
fulled *v.* befouled, spoilt 633.
furth *adv.* forth 515, 783, 784.

G

gay *v.* go 234, 267, 783; **ga** 698; **gase** 934; **gayse** 576; **gane** 830.
gayn *adj.* to hand, near 696.
gan *v.* began 173, 784, **gun** 505, 620, 663.

Select Glossary

gang *v.* go, walk 60.
gapand *v.* gaping 719.
gar *v.* cause to be (*pa. p.*), i.e. with infinitive to form passive 349, 427, 498, &c.; **gartt** 251, 253, 278; cause 376, 1148, 1210; **gartt** 416, 665, 698, 979.
gast *n.* spirit 558, 943, 944, &c.
gastly *adv.* in spirit 172.
gate *n.* way 698.
gedird *v.* gathered 710.
gest *n.* tale, story 36.
gylte *n.* offence, crime 622; ~s 456.
gyrned *v.* grinned, made a face 719.
gytten *v.* gained; **yll**~ ill-gotten 830.
glewmen *n.* minstrels 36.
gnaste *v.* gnashed his teeth 719.
godely *adv.* graciously, abundantly 770, 781.
graffe *n.* grave 934; **grayff** 965; **graue** 1069.
grayn *v.* groan 605.
gramarcy *excl.* many thanks 663; **graunte mercy** 773.
grathe *adj.* prepared, ready 680.
graue see **graffe**.
greff *v.* grieve, annoy 1285; **greues** 569, 997.
grett *v.* weep 605.
greuaunce *n.* trouble, affliction 1272, 1278.
greues see **greff**.
greuouse *adj.* serious, great 456, 622.
gryme *v.* infin. 569 n.
gud *adj.* good, right 61, 147, 1091.

3

ʒhere *n.* year 78, 183, 486, 560; **ʒere** 321, 468; years 717; ~s 1025; **ʒeres** 702; **yeres** 83.
ʒytt *conj.* moreover, still, yet 95, 284, 831, &c.

H

haile *adj.* whole, secure, hale 359, 379, 625, &c.
hald *n.* assistance, support 464.
hald *v.* keep, hold 425, 630, 860, 956; consider 581.

halely *adv.* in devout fashion 1112.
haly *adj.* holy 208, 508, 696, &c.
halynesse *n.* holiness, holy way of life 115, 152, 203, &c.
halowes *n.* saints 1230.
hame *n.* home 582, 587, 626, &c.
hand *n.* possession 1027; **to hys handes** near by 265.
happe *n.* good fortune 813, 1187.
harlott *n.* villain, wretch 681.
haunte *v.* practise, engage in 514; ~**and** 68, 115; ~**d** 152, 203.
he *adj. and adv.* see **heghe**.
heghe *adj.* high, noble, great, tall 115, 392, 631, &c.; **he** 459, 1230; *adv.* **he** high 409.
heght *n.* height; **spake on** ~ spoke loudly 594.
hele *n.* health, well-being 813, 988, 1232.
heled *v.* healed 975.
helefull *adj.* healthy, conducive to well-being 1187.
hend 395 n.
herce *n.* hearse, bier 949.
hertes *n.* harts, stags 631, 652, 660.
hethen *adv.* hence 826, 906.
hew *n.* countenance, appearance 301.
hy *v.* hasten, go 173; ~**ed** 357, 587, 664, &c.
hyde *n.* skin, complexion 301.
hympne *n.* hymn 68; **ympnes** 171, 912.
hyrd *n.* shepherd 1227.
hoge *adj.* great 115.
holett *n.* little cave 388, 453.
honest *adj.* decent 252.
hontt *v.* hunt 357.
horne *n.* horn; **by the** ~ in abundance 782.
hors *n.* horses 463.
houre *n.* hour; **day and** ~ always 24, 763.
house *n.* religious house 121, 1176.
housebandry *n.* agricultural employment, cultivation of the soil 806.
housynge *n.* home, house 366.
hull *n.* mean dwelling 409.

106 Select Glossary

I, Y

yemed v. governed, ordered 83.
yeres see ʒhere.
yha adv. yes 417, 782, 784.
yhates n. gates 1247.
ylkay adj. each, every 1, 533, 727, &c.; ylka 468, 1134, 1274; ~ a 1052; ylk 34, 1078; pron. ilkane each one 729.
yll adv. wrongfully, ill 830; gaffe hym ~ was distressed 925.
ympnes see hympne.
incheson n. reason 1066.
instance n. assiduity 1239.
intentt see ententt.
invy n. envy 154, 674.
yode v. went 128, 561, 778, &c.
irke adj. angry, loath 235 n., 510.
iwys adv. indeed, certainly 249, 545, 788.

L

layn v. be silent about, conceal 309.
lamme n. lambs 666.
lang adv. for a long time 1003.
langir cpt. adv. longer 161, 350, 365.
langor n. disease 1268.
lath n. barn 254, 646, 655.
lathe adj. loathsome, hateful 679.
latt v. allow, let, cause 661.
lawe adj. of low estate, humble 393; adv. low 1067.
lede n. people 1.
leynd v. remain 875; lendys 130.
lele adj. loyal, faithful 4, 227, 527, &c.; trustworthy 572, 832, 1204; adv. loyally 1226.
lendys see leynd.
lere v. learn 77; ~d informed 677; lerred the learned, clergy 889, 1217.
lese v. relieve, loose 1268.
lest sup. adj. least 156.
lett v. hinder 706.
leuenyng n. lightning 1274.
leuer cpt. adj. more pleased 241.
lewed adj. ignorant, lay 102, 889, 1217.
lykkend v. likened 12.

lyfelade n. sustenance, means of living 641.
lyffyng n. life-story 16.
lyght v. relieved, cured 975, 1154.
lyme n. limb 618.
list v. pleases 831.
lyst n. desire 37, 496.
lyth n. joint 618.
lythe n. people 461.
lythe v. listen 432.
lytte n. delay 743.
loued v. praised 671, 1106.
louynge n. praise 901; ~s 1143.
louse v. loose 667.
luffly adj. gracious 1.

M

mace n. club 440; ~s 438.
make v. see maike.
maden n. maiden 81.
may adv. more 75; adj. 93; n. 120.
maike n. equal 895; make 1263.
maike v. make 741, 756, 910, &c.; makys 476; mayd 158, 382, 478, &c.
mayn n. strength 186, 869.
mayned v. maimed, injured 977.
malicoly n. melancholy 1195.
mansiounes n. buildings 253.
manteyn v. support, maintain 793.
mare n. chief officer of a city 218, 486.
mare cpt. adj. greater 134, 367, 591, &c.; adv. more 742, 849, 920, &c.; mair rather 225; n. more 78; mair 1125.
mased v. bewildered 158.
mast sup. adj. greatest 473, 1175, 1259, &c.; sup. adv. most 6, 752, 1202.
mekyll adj. great 241, 658, 893, 947; much 790.
mede n. reward (in heaven) 1190, 1200.
mele n. meal 274.
melle v. speak 571, 831.
menbirs n. limbs 977.
menged v. mingled, mixed 1138.
menʒhe n. community, household 1038.

Select Glossary

merred *v.* disturbed, troubled 477, 882; confounded 158, 1292; wicked 244.
mesor *n.* moderation 275, 284, 293; ~es measures, quantities 311.
messy *n.* mass 238; **messe** 1099.
messy *n.* mercy 473.
mett *v.* meet 64, 606, 1247.
mette *n.* food 206, 259.
mettes *n.* measurements 311.
mynd *n.* intention 160.
mynne *v.* remember, consider 238, 1210.
mynne *cpt. adj.* less; **mare and** ~ all 134, 220.
myscheffe *n.* trouble 882; ~ys 1284.
myscomforth *n.* discomfort, unhappiness 1292.
mysse *v.* lack 472.
mode *n.* temper, mood, disposition 59, 127, 378, &c.
mody *adj.* stately 177.
modynesse *n.* greatness of spirit 124.
moysand *v.* musing 433.
morne *n.* morning; **euen and** ~ always 637.
mostre *v.* show, display 894.
motte *v.* must; **so** ~ **I the** so help me 599, 761.
mowed *v.* moved 742; jumped about 704.

N

nane *pron.* no one 71, 910, 958; **nayne** 803; none 169.
nedder *n.* serpent 692.
neuen *v.* tell 627.
newed *v.* brought forth, produced 818.
nyll *v.* will not 370, 812.
noght *neg. adv.* not 44, 94, 212, &c.; **nott** 472, 776; *pron.* nought, nothing 378, 756, 828, 1086.
noy *n.* affliction, distress 402, 1288.
noyes *v.* annoys, distresses 443; ~and 692.
nouther *adv.* neither 65, 907.

O

okir *n.* usury 312.
oght *adv.* in any way 755.
or *adv.* before 778, 842.
orysoune *n.* prayer 68; ~ons 740 1005.
ouersett *v.* overcome 725, 1198
outher *conj.* either 1285.
outt *prep.* out; **boght** ~ ransomed 1118.

P

page *n.* youth, lad 98.
payd *v.* satisfied, contented, pleased 520, 635, 644.
paile *adj.* pale 301.
payres *v.* despoils, harms 998.
pamentt *n.* stone floor, hard surface 262.
Pape *n.* Pope 1089, 1099, 1105; ~ys 1000.
paramoure *adv.* for love's sake 4; *n.* paramours lovers 42.
pareles *n.* perils, dangers 1293; per~ 1304.
parle *v.* speak 694.
past *n.* paste 276.
patrone *n.* patron saint, ? founder 990, 1132, 1167.
pece *n.* peace, tranquillity 1241.
peirles *adj.* matchless, peerless 210, 1167.
pere *n.* man of high rank 1132.
pereles see **pareles**.
persayued *v.* perceived, understood 906.
persone *n.* rector, parson 807, 811, 821.
phannoune *n.* maniple 92.
pyke *n.* pitch 694.
pykes *n.* spikes 435.
pynde *v.* shut up, impound 647; impounded, imprisoned 655.
pyne *n.* pain, torment 904, 1297.
pyned *v.* tormented 1044.
play *v.* sport, desport oneself 334.
playn *adj.* open; ~ **batayll** fair fight, open battle 58.
playng *n.* pleasure 525.

playntte n. accusation, charge, complaint 689, 822, 1311.
plyghte n. sin, sinful state 700, 992; ~s 1293.
ploghe n. plough 267, 660, 791, &c.; ~s 1047.
plonged v. forced, driven 1117.
poralles n. poor men 184, 779.
potage n. soup, stew 277.
pouerte n. poverty 526, 1295; ~uertt 826.
preciouse adj. excellent 1087.
prese n. battle 40.
presidentt n. abbot, head of house 113, 1183.
prest n. priest 90.
prest v. compelled 401.
preste adj. ready, prepared 706.
priuely adv. secretly, privately 213.
proffe v. try, prove 9, 108.
prophetised v. prophesied 861.
proporciond v. adjusted, proportioned 276.
purueaunce n. provisions, goods 190.

Q

quod v. said 782.
quayntte adj. sly, cunning 531.

R

rayked v. went 583, 794.
rayd v. rode 839, 853.
rayse v. rose 200, 410, 549, &c.; rase 747.
rare v. yell, shout 608.
rased v. restored to life 984; **raysed** produced, raised 1039.
raued v. wandered, strayed 578.
raunsoun n. ransom 1051.
raunsoune v. ransom 1123.
rebelloure n. rebel 339.
reke see **reike**.
reken adj. ready 687.
receptour n. receiver 345.
rede n. reason, judgment 924.
redy adj. ready 315, 536; nearest 664.
reike n. smoke 410; **reke** 412.

relese v. release 1041.
religioune n. religious order 107, 962; ~s those under a religious vow 1036.
remed v. lamented 307.
repentt v. was sorrowful, sad 239 n.
resaued v. received, welcomed 217, 1090.
reue v. seize 953.
reued v. ? dwelt 126 n.
reuffully adv. dolefully, sorrowfully 608.
reul v. rule, order 1180; **rewled** 87, 294; **rouled** 900.
rewes v. grieves 491; **rewe** have pity on 621; ~ed sorrowed, lamented 239, 307.
rewle n. rule (religious), way of life 107, 877.
ryall adj. invested through or with royal power 407, 1036.
ryally adv. royally, magnificently 839.
ryffe adv. frequently, often 969.
ryghtwys adj. righteous, just, upright 48, 97, 905, &c.
ryghtwislye adv. righteously, justly 1180.
rysshe n. rush, tittle, something insignificant 884.
ryst v. rested; ~ **hym** dwelt 509.
roch n. rock, cliff 140, 168; ~es 459.
Rode n. Cross 508, 966, 1074.
rodely adv. roughly 808.
romaunce n. ? French 899 n.
rosed v. praised, extolled 209.
rouled see **reul**.
routte n. company, body 233, 955.
rupe v. shout loudly 608.
rusty adj. wretched 726 n.

S

sakles adj. innocent 611.
sadde adj. resolute 880.
sadly adv. seriously, with determination 260, 911.
saffly adv. safely 798.
saike n. sake 254, 443, 896, &c.
sayff adj. safe, secure 910 n.

Select Glossary

saylle *n.* soul 767.
saynd *v.* signed, marked with the sign of the Cross 978.
sair *adv.* sorely 239, 307; **sare** 491.
salde *v.* sold 611.
sall *v.* shall 324, 402, 518, &c.; **sulde** 364, 421, 426; **suld** used to 259; **suld** had to 864, 928, 941; **suld** ought to 1094.
salussed *v.* greeted 104, 490.
sammenn *adv.* together 866.
sare *adj.* grievous 919.
sare *adv.* see **sair**.
sauyng *n.* salvation, deliverance 1190.
saule *n.* soul 167, 320, 880, &c.; ~s 903, 930, 1178.
sause *n.* appetizer, relish 685.
sawe *n.* decree 649.
sawe *v.* sow 1048.
skathe *n.* harm, injury 351, 645, 656.
skathe *v.* harm, injure 426, 1285.
skerre *n.* rock, cliff 19.
schrewes *n.* evil persons 62.
scoles *n.* schools, classes 77.
screde *n.* strip, rag 604.
scriptur *n.* account, story 266.
seke *adj.* sick 971.
sekerly *adv.* surely, without doubt 498; **sykyrly** 1024.
seknes *n.* illness 919, 987, 1299.
sege *n.* throne 8.
seyne *adj. and v.* seen, visible 648, 800, 1082, 1152.
selcouth *adv.* seldom 800.
sen *conj.* since 1174, 1222, 1252.
sentence *n.* opinion 1078.
sere *adj.* separate, divers 70, 435, 999, &c.; *adv.* separately 729.
seryne 1218 n.
serse *v.* search out, look for 505.
sesed *v.* ceased, stopped 707.
sexten *num.* sixteen 717.
shente *v.* disgraced, confounded 541.
shontt *v.* push 722.
shwed *v.* shown 1218 n.
sykyrly see **sekerly**.
simple *adj.* humble 1182, 1236.

systers *n.* sisters in God, nuns 1218.
syte *n.* sorrow, pain 1299.
sithen *adv.* afterwards 1048.
slake *n.* ditch 544.
slegh *adj.* cunning 725.
slyke *adj.* such 44, 580, 756, &c.
slokkend *v.* extinguished 714.
snawe *n.* snow 561, 1068.
sobyr *adj.* steadfast 1205.
sodann *adj.* sudden 1275.
soyne *adv.* immediately, soon 147.
solitary *adj.* solitary, hermit 24.
sotell *adj.* cunning 531, 597.
soth *n.* truth 271, 499.
sothely *adv.* indeed, truly 7, 815.
sothen *v.* cooked 279.
soule *n.* relish 685.
soumbe *v.* count, reckon 968.
space *n.* time 263, 825; place 336.
spelunke *n.* cave 493.
spirred *v.* asked 335.
stalworth *adj.* sturdy, resolute 54.
stalworthly *adv.* valiantly 193, 377, 870.
stand *v.* stand; ~ **in sted** prevail 938; ~ **agayn** oppose 870.
sted *n.* place 299, 881, 938, &c.
steren *adj.* stern 374.
sterne *n.* star 228.
sty *n.* path; **bath by** ~ **and strette** everywhere, all over 634.
stythe *adj.* brave, valiant 1215.
stythely *adv.* boldly 439.
stray *n.* straw 710.
strand *n.* shore; **ouer streme and** ~ everywhere 1113.
strenkell *n.* water-sprinkler 695.
stryde *n.* stride; **stire hym halffe a** ~ move him an inch 887.
stroede *v.* spoilt, trampled on 634.
subieccioune *n.* obedience 1018.
sufferaunce *n.* endurance 1243.
suffraynge *n.* king 757; ~**rayne** 764, 908.
suffrandly *adv.* specially 1191.
sulped *v.* polluted 1153.
sute *n.* soot 1153.
sway *adv.* so, thus 80, 114, 158, &c.; **swa** 205, 261.

110 Select Glossary

sweltt *v.* died 943; dead 865.
swylk *adj.* such 149.
swyth *adv.* quickly 251, 324.

T, þ

ta *v.* take 268; **tane** 1312.
taynte *n.* disgrace, blemish 532, 690, 1312.
teynde *n.* tithe 809; ~s 816, 819.
teyne *v.* annoy, vex 676.
teyne *n.* harm 799, 1289.
tenementt *n.* house 524.
tentt *v.* listen to, attend to 303.
texte *n.* story, book 327.
þaretyll *adv.* thereto; **grauntte** ~ agree to it 770; near 179.
the *v.* prosper 599, 761.
thewes *n.* manners, habits 61.
þider *adv.* thither, to that place 583, 952.
tholemode *adj.* patient 1197.
thonour *n.* thunder 1274.
threst *n.* thirst 1294.
threte *n.* threat, threatening 362.
thretyng *n.* threats, threatenings 1283.
thretten *num.* thirteen 469, 472.
thryffe *v.* thrive, prosper 80; **thryue** 776.
thrugh *adv.* through; **by and** ~ always 135.
tyfeld *v.* disordered 684.
tyll *prep.* to 369, 589.
type *n.* trick 676.
tyte *adv.* quickly 744, 931, 1103, &c.
to *prep.* as far as 460; in accordance with 1181; *adv.* till 422, 450, 550, &c.
togedir *adv.* together 269, 560, 710.
toghe *adj.* strong, diligent; **mayd hym** ~ was persistent 805.
toyled *v.* distressed, wearied 821.
toumbe *n.* tomb 967, 974.
tour *n.* tower, castle 371, 524; **tow(r)e** 142 n.
trace *n.* way; **toke** ~ made his way 530.
traye *n.* affliction 1280.
trayle *n.* sledge 435.

trayne *n.* stratagem 597.
trispas *n.* sin, trespass 71, 1146, 1302, 1311.
tryst *n.* trust, faith 1175.
trow *v.* believe 572, 832.
tway *num.* two 125, 438, 463, &c.; **twa** 1083.

V

vanist *v.* vanished, disappeared 449.
vmbeseged *v.* attacked, assailed 728.
vmbythoght *v.* bethought 511.
vncled *v.* undressed 429.
vnconnandly *adv.* unskilfully, roughly, wrongfully 819.
vndirtoke *v.* learnt 1081.
vnfrely *adj.* ugly 194.
vnhappes *n.* misfortunes 1287.
vnlele *adv.* unlawfully 311, 827.
vnmeke *adj.* proud, arrogant 231.
vnmyld *adj.* fierce 244.
vntrewly *adv.* unlawfully 816.
vnwarly *adv.* incautiously, carelessly 542.
vnwettand *v.* ignorant 134.
voyce *n.* voice 396; **voce** 1248.
voyde *v.* remove 1212.
vse *v.* practice 1211; ~**and** 69, 205.
vthir *adj.* other 312, 892, 1240, 1282; *pron.* 313.

W

wafull *adj.* wretched, unhappy 1260.
wagged *v.* shook 653.
way *n.* sorrow, misery 948, 1215, 1260, 1291; *adj.* angry, wretched 545, 709.
waike *adj.* weak, feeble 797.
wald *v.* wished 66, 541, 777, 837; used to 258, 260, 261, 974.
waloway *excl.* alas, alack 552; *adv.* wretchedly 724.
wandreth *n.* unhappiness, misery 1291.
wane *n.* dwelling, home 829.
wane *v.* decrease 325; ~**d** grew pale 261.

Select Glossary

waned *v.* lamented 540.
wanyng *n.* lessening 697.
wanton *adj.* undisciplined 65.
wapped *v.* wrapped, dressed 603.
wardan *n.* protector, guardian 478.
warld see werld.
warlow *n.* supernatural being 709; ~es 449.
wate *n.* water, liquid 697.
wede *n.* garment 603.
wey⟨n⟩dynge *n.* departure 917.
weile *adv.* well 1151.
weyn *n.* doubt 1151.
weynd *v.* go, depart 784, 837, 928, 1162.
weyne *v.* guess, think 405.
well *n.* good fortune 886, 1215.
were *v.* protect 1260.
werld *n.* world, life 478, 900, 1084, &c.; warld 856; warlde worldly temptations 56, 1213.
wex *v.* grew, became 419, 675, 709, &c.
whedir *conj.* whether 281, 370; *pron.* whichever of two 1271.
whike see whilk.
whider *adv.* whithersoever 1270.
whilk *pron.* which 27; whike 1009.
while *n.* time 130, 329, 403, &c.; on a wyle once 601.
wyght *n.* person, creature 1260.
wyght *adj.* brave, valiant 54.
wyghtly *adv.* exceedingly 318.
wyld *adj.* wild (animal) 243, 581, 1281; wayward 65; *n.* wild animals 346, 418.
wyle see while.
wille *adj.* demented; ~ he wex ...

off hys rede he did not know what to do 924.
wylled *v.* inclined 1144.
wype *n.* lapwing 675 n.
wyrke *v.* perform, work 590, 1144.
wirkes *v.* suffers pain 796.
wyrshype *n.* worship, reverence 481, 886.
wyse *n.* way, manner 462, 837, 1122, 1249.
wyse *adj.* sane 982.
wyshe *v.* guide 917; wyssed 135.
wyttles *adj.* crazy, mad 540, 578, 584, 980; furious 419.
wytt *v.* know 1034; waytt 95, 96, 1151; wyste 250, 503, 635, &c.
wytte *n.* understanding 14, 765; wits, right mind 980. '
wode *adj.* mad, insane 419, 584, 980.
won *v.* dwell, live 501, 512, 526, 980; woune 149, 1163; wounes 344, 1169; wouned 151, 174, 183, &c.; wontt 358; ~ed 1084; wontt accustomed 721.
worthly *adj.* noble 329.
wounyng *n.* dwelling 214, 874.
wrang *v.* wrung 318.
wrath *adj.* angry 235; wreth 675.
wreke *n.* vengeance, retribution 619, 823.
wreche *n.* wretch, despicable person 162, 688.
wreth *adj.* see wrath.
wreth *n.* anger 1303.
wrytt *v.* write 862; wrayt 1088; wretyn 730, 1059.

SELECT PROPER NAMES

Bryane Brian de L'Isle or de Insula 737 n., 835, 851, &c.
Knaresburgh Knaresborough in the West Riding of Yorkshire 19, 136, 487, &c.; the people of Knaresborough 954.
Couerham Coverham Abbey in the North Riding of Yorkshire 1022 n.

Flos, Toccus Took Flower, father of St. Robert, 49 n.
Fountaunce Fountains Abbey in the West Riding of Yorkshire 866 n., 931; monks of Fountains Abbey 951.
Gerrard the Devil or a devil 715; Sir Gerrard 698 n.

Grymbalde Kyrkstane Grimbald Church Stone 460 n.
Hedlay Hedley, a cell of Holy Trinity, York, 216 n.
Yue Yve, Robert's companion, 516 n., 527, 558, &c.
Newmostres Newminster 100 n.
Robynett diminutive of Robert 400, 726.
Sayntt Gyle St. Giles 385.
Sayntt Hylde St. Hild 178 n., 240, 567.

Scutivyle, William William de Stuteville 330 n., 404.
Spofford Spofforth in the West Riding of Yorkshire 201 n.
Suniuyte Sunniva, mother of St. Robert, 51 n.
Toccus see **Flos**.
Walter Walter, brother of St. Robert, 485 n., 503, 505, 970.
William William de Stuteville 333, 411, 433 &c.

APPENDIXES

In the Latin texts which are printed below the following practices have been observed. The final readings of the manuscripts are presented; that is, if a later hand has supplied a word or letter obviously missing from the original text, that word or letter is included below. No drastic emendations have been undertaken, and, consequently, one or two passages, of which the meaning is in doubt, have been left unaltered. Missing letters are supplied in brackets, thus—infam⟨i⟩am; otherwise emendations are given in the text and the manuscript readings are relegated to footnotes. (?) indicates a doubtful reading. The punctuation has been modernized.

The edition by the Reverend Paul Grosjean in *Analecta Bollandiana*, lvii. 364–400, of the Latin lives of St. Robert, given in a slightly shortened form here in Appendixes A and B, has been a valuable guide in the transcription and punctuation of these texts.

APPENDIX A

The following Latin prose life of St. Robert is contained in the British Museum Manuscript, Egerton 3143, ff. 15^r–31^v. The prologue and epilogue are omitted since they have no bearing on *M*.

1. *De ortu et parentela Sancti Roberti Knaresburgensis. Capitulum* f. 16^v *primum*. Sanctus Robertus iuxta Knaresburgum, nacione Anglicus, a preclaris parentibus originem duxit. Extitit in civitate Eboracensi oriundus, patre videlicet Tocco Flore, matre vero Siminima nomine, qui inter nobiliores dicte civitatis preclari extiterunt, christianissimam vitam sequi decreverunt. Inter quos filium genuerunt cui nomen Robertus imposuerunt, et educaverunt gracia et virtute. Adultum autem moribus et sciencia cum singulis virtutibus instruxerunt. Qui quidem cepit bone indolis esse. Nullius profecto lascivie sive inquietudinis[1] animum exercicio dedit. Crebris in oracionibus ac in omnibus aliis sanctitatis studiis se frequentabat. Nulli uncquam voluptati se subdidit. Sic ornatus adolescens undique virtutibus ac Spiritus Sancti gracia perfusus intusque illustratus et inspiratus, cepit in perfeccione Dei perfectissimus esse. Sepe ecclesias sive monasteria Robertus sepius frequentabat et proponebat animo electus adolescens in ordine sacerdocii Deo devocius deservire, sed quid eum ab hoc incepto proposito retraxit, penitus ignoro. Ergo Deo totum committimus, cui nullum latet secretum, melius quam nostris ignoranciis aliquid temere diffinire. Unde iste vir Deo devotus, episcopo declinans, ordinem subdiaconi sibi dare cum instancia postulavit; cui benigne episcopus annuebat, et manu episcopali ordinatus, maturo gressu f. 17 recedebat.

[1] inequitudinis.

114   *Appendix A*

2. *Quomodo Robertus ivit ad Novum Monasterium ad fratrem ibidem conversantem. Capitulum secundum.* Post aliquod tempus elapsum, Robertus occidentales secessit in partes, sic ducendo[1] ad quoddam monasterium vocatum Novum Monasterium, ordinis Cisterciensis, in quo fratrem habuit conversum, utpote minus litteratum, sed conversacione precipuum. Mutua facta salutacione inter Robertum et fratrem illius monasterii conversum, ait frater, 'Scalam perfeccionis et virtutis ingredere devotus, ubi regulas spirituales et sanctorum sancciones discas discipline.' Auditis monitis salutaribus, ab abbate et dicti loci fratribus est gratanter acceptus. Videns autem abbas eius perfectissimam conversacionem[2] ac mirabilia que per eum Dominus ostendere est dignatus, ait, 'O religiosi, celi volatilia attendite quomodo huic obediunt, et quomodo Robertus carnem macerat, mundi cuncta declinans oblectamenta.' Quatuor mensibus et una quindena completis, Spiritu Sancto revelante, ad parentes priores Robertus est reversus.

3. *Qualiter devenit Knaresburgo ad heremitam. Capitulum tercium.* Elapsis autem diebus paucis, parentibus inconsultis, vir Deo devotus confugit, divina inspiracione vocatus, Knaresburgo ad heremitam quendam vitam arciorem sub rupe ducentem, secum in consorcio
f. 17ᵛ eligens habitare. Viso autem ab heremita[3] Roberto et honestate qua decuit recepto, ait heremita, 'Gracias omnipotenti Deo refero, qui mihi collegam strenu⟨u⟩m ac devotissimum transmittere est dignatus'. Nam post hoc per aliquod temporis intervallum, milite heremita, instigante diabolo, tanquam canis ad vomitum, ad uxorem et filios reverso, Robertus solus remansit omni humano solacio destitutus, ubi miris abstinenciis carnem macerabat. Postea autem abiit Robertus ad quandam devotam matronam non procul a cella, cuius fama pluribus applaudebat, ab ea elimosinam petiturus, dicens, 'O mulier Deo devota, de tua substancia mihi libenter elimosinam elargiri digneris.' Que ait, 'Do tibi capellam Sancte Hylde virginis, et de terra adiacente quantum tibi fodere complacebit.' Accepta itaque elimosina, ibidem Robertus fere per annum carnem suam continua pena affligens solus remanebat; contemplacioni divine et aliarum virtutum exercicio vacans, Domino complacebat.

4. *Quomodo latrones eum de alimentis spoliaverunt. Capitulum quartum.* Quodam autem tempore, dum vir Dei in oracionibus et aliis sacris meditacionibus immobilis pernoctavit, latrones ad eum divertentes eius cellam fregerunt et pauperum alimenta, videlicet panem, caseum, cum hiis similia rapuerunt, et tunc cum omni festinancia abire sunt conati. Non enim vir Dei propter hoc turbatur, sciens misericordiam Dei in temptacionibus semper adesse, sed pocius memor illius evangelii, sic dicens, 'Si vos persecuti sunt homines in
f. 18 una civitate, fugite ad aliam.' Tunc autem, ab eo loco fugiens, ad

---

[1] *Read* secedendo?   [2] conversacioni.   [3] heremitam.

Appendix A

villam de Spofford in animo ire proponebat, ubi aliquandiu moram tenens, in oracionibus et aliis affliccionibus vacans prolixius persistebat. Cuius sanctitatis fama[1] crebrescente, multitudo circumiacentis patrie ad eum contuendum catervatim confluebat et eidem tanquam sancto[2] laudes et honores satis optulerunt. Unde vir sanctus, semper vanam gloriam respuens, clam dis⟨c⟩essit, nec ibidem remanere voluit.

5. *Quomodo Hedelay declinavit; vir monachus est effectus. Capitulum quintum.* Audito enim de Roberti recessu, invitatus est et rogatus a monachis de Hedlay ut cum eis remaneret. Quod vir Dei modeste annuit, ac eorum collegio se humiliter sociavit et cum eis discipul⟨in⟩is spiritualibus se mancipavit. Erat enim huius modestissimi viri indumentum, quo indutus erat, una solummodo alba cuculla, que pocius nuditatem corporis cooperiret quam vitali corpori calorem exhiberet. Panis vero eius de quatuor partibus farine ordiacie et quinta cineris cribro proporcionaliter commixtis[3] conficiebatur. Carnes quoque coctas sive assatas,[4] gustato sapore, cito repellebat. Pulmentum de incrudis eleorum[5] foliis vell fabarum modicum, adiecto sale, sibi condiebatur. Farinula semel in ebdomata tamen eis infusa fuit. O vos delicati viri, qui omne genus vestiment⟨or⟩um[6] superbiendo queritis, et ventres vestros cibis et potibus[7] delicatis reficitis et excessivis, huius sancti viri vestitus simplicitatem ac cibariorum insipiditatem ante mentis occulos ponite.[8] Demum Robertus, vir modestus ac mitis, f. 18ᵛ cuius conversacio cum celi senatoribus extitit—semper enim celestia sapiebat et non que super terram—perversis[9] dissolutisque in omnibus displicebat, habens in me⟨mo⟩ria illud Pauli qui dicit, 'Si hominibus placerem, Cristi servus non essem.' Monachos de suis[10] insolenciis palam arguebat. Unde ab eisdem dissolute viventibus et sue sanctissime conversacioni invidentibus inpugnatus, ad capellam Sancte Hilde virginis, ubi prius habitavit, denuo est reversus, mallens in herimo cum feris in furoribus habitare quam cum fratribus malignis et sibi expugnantibus;[11] quia secundum Pauli se⟨n⟩tenciam periculum est in falsis fratribus.

6. *Quomodo secundo ad cappellam Beate Hilde revenit. Capitulum sextum.* Reversus est ilico Robertus ad priorem locum habitare. De cuius glorioso adventu beata matrona supra memorata plurimum congaudebat. Que, postposita dilacione, conductis artificibus, ceteris necessariis ac orreis[12] pro frugibus reponendis.[13] Vaniloquia vero hospitum ac serviencium ubique declinavit, et precipue dum cibum sumere consuevit. In oracionibus et vigiliis crebris sepius pernoctavit. Sompnum ad mensuram capiens, se prostravit pavimento. Quatuor autem habens famulos,[14] duos pro agriculture operibus deputavit; tercium

[1] fame.   [2] sanctum.   [3] commixter.   [4] assatatas.
[5] *Read* aleorum *or* olerum?   [6] vistimentum.   [7] potabus.   [8] posite.
[9] perversus.   [10] eius.   [11] expungnantibus.   [12] orrium.   [13] *Verb &c. omitted.*   [14] familos.

vero pro aliis necessariis alibi faciendis retinuit. Quartum utique secum tenuit perambulando patriam pro elimosinis fidelium pauperibus et egenis, quos sibi congregavit, sollicite colligendis.

f. 19   7. *Quomodo mater eius defuncta eidem dormienti apparuit. Capitulum septimum.* Conti⟨n⟩gebat quoque quodam die Roberto in ameno prato inter redolentes flosculos dormienti, mater eius nuper defuncta tota tristis, pallida ac deformis apparere, dicens se pro usuris et mensuris aliis⟨que⟩ malificiis, quibus vivens usa est, penis pregravibus deputari, nisi eius piissimis precibus Domino pro ea fusis subvenire dignaretur. Cui Robertus, matris mesticia vehementer motus, facere repromisit. Deprecante autem Roberto Dominum per totum anni circulum pro matre fusis lacrimis, tandem a Domino exauditus est, secundum illam Domini sentenciam quam dixit discipulis suis, 'Quodcumque pecieritis in nomine meo, dabit vobis.' Iterum autem, ut profertur,[1] dormitanti Roberto mater eius facie serena vultuque letabundo apparuit, inmensas Deo et filio gracias agens ac benedicens, se ad sempiternam requiem dixit pervenire.

8. *Quomodo dominus Willelmus de Scutivilla prostravit habitacula. Capitulum octavum.* Probatus itaque vir Dei Robertus, ut superius dictum est, et in proposito iam per omnia dignus inventus, ut eciam secundum hoc evidencior super eum divine providencie opperacio appareret, iuxta illud quod scriptum est, 'Qui diligit filium suum, assiduat illi flagella', repetitur adhuc examine maioris temptacionis exquirendus.[2] Nam cum post hoc incredibili se ieiunio et abstinencia maceraret, die nocteque vigiliis et oracionibus insistendo accidit die quadam quendam dominum Willelmum de Scutivilla, dominatorem terre, per cellam suam casu pervenire. Cernens autem eius edificia, et

f. 19v cuius hec essent diligenter inquirebat. Cui famuli dixerunt quod quidam heremita, Robertus nomine, Deo devotissimus, ibidem habitabat. Ad quos Willelmus animo perturbatus, invidia diabolica stimulatus, ait, 'Nequaquam, sed hic furum et latronum fautor est et receptor.' Tunc iuravit per occulos Dei quod eum a foresta sua exppelleret, nec eum ulterius ibidem habitare sineret. Sic servis suis minaciter prorumpebat, 'O satellites, quantocius hunc Robertum ypocritam expellite; simul eius edificia funditus subvertite. Quod si exire contempserit, ipsum vivum ignibus curate concremare.' Satellites profecto indiscretum imperium principis discrete dissimulantes implere noluerunt.[3] Post aliquot autem dies elapsas, idem Willelmus, velut leo pre furore ire fremens, est reversus, vidensque servientes imperium suum minus peregisse[4] et ad effectum minime perduxisse, ait, 'Per occulos Dei, vestros occulos eruam si ulterius imperium differatis.' Satellites vero, domini sui manus ultrices timentes, Roberti servi Dei benignissimi edificia terre funditus coequarunt. Videns autem vir modestus tribulaciones succrescere et angustias varias sibi

[1] prefertur.   [2] exquiretur.   [3] voluerunt.   [4] peragisse.

ex adverso accidere, quas humani generis hostis callidus adversus
eum excitaverat, et prostrata habitacula, prorupit in hec verba,
'Renunciate domino vestro quia, nollit velit, tabernacula iuxta tur-
rim suam in eternum sive eum[1] fixurus, malicias eius sive minas
minime metuendo. Quia Dominus est mihi protector, idio non timebo
quid faciat mihi homo.'

9. *Quomodo ad capellam Sancti Egidii est reversus. Capitulum no-* f. 20
num. Abhinc declinabat ad locum ubi prius habitaverat iuxta Knaresburgum. Nullam ibi habitacionem[2] inveniens preter capellam Sancti
Egidii, de pa⟨u⟩xillis ramusculis rupi annexis ibidem sibi modicum[3]
tugurium[4] construebat, in quo quiecius Dominum contemplando
vacaret et plebis strepitum ubique declinaret. Multa de tanto patre
narrari possunt, sed (?) tamen plurima pretermittuntur, quia non
contingit uni alicui scire cuncta que per illum Deus operatus est.
Erat enim vera lucerna ardens satis temporibus modernis spectabilis,
lumen non sub modio sed super montem positum, ut qui ingrediuntur
lumen veritatis palam queant intueri. Dispersa itaque sanctitatis fama
Roberti longe late in provincia, ad eum tam nobiles quam ignobiles
utriusque sexus confluebant munera sibi differentes, eius asspectu
letificati ac colloquio edificati et in amore Cristi radicati recesserunt.
Agellum inter rupem et flumen ad virtutem[5] viri Dei populus[6] suis
propriis colendum[7] carucis tradiderunt. Post hec autem a quodam
fide digno ut asseritur,[8] audivit demonem lugubri voce clamantem et
dicentem, 'Heu! heu! hominem de paradisi gaudiis deieci, hunc autem
Robertum inopem et inermem convincere non valeo.' Sic dolebat
humane salutis adversarius Dei famulum non prevaluisse et a fragili
corpore se tociens fuisse superatum, quia maior est eius versucie et
subtilitatis arrogancia quam fortitudo. Quid igitur, o lector, de f. 20ᵛ
homine hoc animadvertendum est? Nunquid spiritibus inmundis
subtili examinacione obviare potuit, nisi Sancti Spiritus infusio et
gracia superhabundans eum docuisset?

10. *Quomodo dictus Willelmus precepit prosterni idem habitaculum.*
Capitulum decimum. Artificiosa demonis huius calliditate iniquitatis
ipse demon, tocius quietis inpaciens et pacis quieti nullatenus adquiescens,[9] cum locum sue seduccionis apud Robertum nullum haberet, volatu facilis, sicut levis est velocitate naturali, exiit et, ut prius,
excitavit dictum dominum Willelmum adversum famulum Dei Robertum ut sic eum callide precipitaret. Non longe post, adveniens
Willelmus de Scutivilla de australi parte et die quadam casu iuxta
Roberti cavernaculam pergens, vaporem[10] fumi in sublime tenden-
tem[11] a domo Roberti, quam noviter construebat, conspexit. Quid
ille vapor fumi pretenderet sollicite requirebat.[12] Cui responderunt

[1] (s.e.) *Read* sum?   [2] habitacioni.   [3] modicam.   [4] turgurim.
[5] virtutum.   [6] populis.   [7] colem.   [8] asseruit ut.
[9] adquiessens.   [10] vaporemque.   [11] tendentes.   [12] requirebant.

118 Appendix A

astantes hunc esse Roberti heremite de domuncula[1] in divinis habitantis. 'An,' inquid Willelmus, 'hic idem est quem de foresta mea, prostratis habitaculis, expellere feci?' Dicunt, 'Sic utique.' Tunc enim turbatus animo Willelmus iuravit, 'Per occ⟨u⟩los Dei, sompnum occulis meis non dabo priusquam istius Roberti tabernaculum funditus evertam.' Sed pro nocturnis tenebris quod vovit perficere non valuit; sed domum veniens et cum incaluisset mero, iuravit in crastino se Robertum a domicilio penitus expulsurum. Dormiente dicto Willelmo in cubili, apparuerunt ei tres viri terribili et horribili aspectu, fuligine nigriores, quorum duo, traham ferream igne flammantem deportantes asperimis aculeis ardentibus plenam, lateribus dormientis incusserunt; tercius vero, vir procere stature, duas clavas ferreas manibus ferens, ad cubile militis cum impetu accessit, dicens, 'Crudelis princeps et diaboli instrumentum, surge velocius et alteram clavam accipe, ac propriam cervicem defende propter iniurias quas viro Dei inferre satagis, quia tecum pro eo pugnaturus huc missus sum.' Attonitus autem animo et territus Willelmus, expansis in altum manibus, exclamavit, dicens, 'Miserere mei, o homo, et parce anime mee. Promitto me omnia dampna per me sibi nequiter illata quantocius emendare et ulterius nunquam iterare.' Et confestim ab eius occulis tota terribilis visio horribilium hominum evanuit. Tunc autem Willelmus in mente sedulus revolvebat quod hec revelacio a Deo facta est propter tirannidem quam Roberto, Dei famulo, facere proponebat. Sed inmensas Deo gracias referebat eo quod ad effectum hec terribilis visio venire non sinebat. Sic enim prince⟨p⟩s divinitus est correptus. De lupo factus est agnus, de persecutore protector, et quem prius expugnaverat, postea genu curvato humiliter adoravit. Mane autem facto, surrexit et cum omni festinancia ad domunculam[2] Roberti, viri Dei, humiliter et devote accessit. Viso vero famulo Dei Roberto, Willelmus, flexis genibus manibusque in altum expansis, cum gemitu ait, 'O Roberte, Deo dilecte, ne reminiscaris iniquitatum mearum quas tibi prius, nesciens tuam sanctitatem, nequeter perpetravi. Meserere mei veniam postulantis et amplius perpetrata emendare proponentis.' Exposita viro Dei tota predicta visio⟨ne⟩, ait, 'Remittat tibi Dominus, dator venie et indulgencie, quicquid mihi deliquisti.' Et erexit eum de terra, dicens, 'Accede, Willelme, ad pacis osculum.' Quod et factum est. Tunc Wyllelmus mero motu Roberto contulit totum et quicquid terre quod continetur inter rupem et Grymbald Kyrkestane in perpetuam elimosinam, et, ut terra inculta non iaceret, duos boves cum duobus equis et totidem vaccis ilico conferebat. Dedit eciam ei singulis annis successivis a festo Nativitatis dominice usque in crastinum Epiphanie Domini alimenta pro tresdecim egenorum pauperum sustentacione et cum aliis infinitis elimosinis pauperibus suis erogandis penuria[3] pregravatis. O stupenda mutacio dextere

[1] dominucula. [2] dominuculam. [3] penuriam.

Appendix A

excelsi! Nam Roberti humilitate et sanctitate mutatur seviens in sanctitatem, tirannus in tutorem, derisor in defensorem et persecutor in protectorem et in coadiutorem famuli Dei Roberti.

11. *Quomodo Walterus, frater eius, edificavit sibi capellam cum cellula. Capitulum undecimum.* Erat enim severus in corripiendo et blandus in eloquio, et cum multi iam ad eum confluebantt, totum spiritum eorum, docente Spiritu Sancto, exhauriebat[1] ut, evacuato f. 22 spiritu superbie, idem Spiritus Sanctus in eis locum melius inveniret.[2] De corporalibus cura, preter de pauperibus, vix aliqua erat. Universum vero eius studium ad spiritualia contulerat scripturas divinas sequi et Cristum ducem habere. Eo autem tempore, fama creberime et celiberime ob insignia tanti hominis percurrente, Walterus, frater Roberti et maior civitatis Eboracensis, accessit ad eum eo quod de eo multa audisset; sed cum adhuc maiora, Spiritu Sancto perdocente, qui per eum operabatur, invenisset, ait, 'Dulc⟨issim⟩e frater Roberte, habitacio tua est nimis arta et angusta et omnimodis commoditatibus inanis et sterilis, et ab hoc ulterius in ea non debes remanere. Si autem meo consilio adquiescens[3] abhinc discedere volueris, collegio quorumcunque regulariter vivencium, ubicumque tibi locum elegeris,[4] te honeste associabo.' Cui vir Dei, constantissimus in proposito incepto, respondit, 'Hec requies mea in seculum seculi; hic habitabo, quoniam elegi eam.' Videns autem Walterus frater Roberti constanciam et quod nullo modo sibi consentire voluit, reversus est Eboracum; a quo quidem missi sunt artifices arcium diversarum, ut Sancte Crucis capellulam ibide⟨m⟩ construere niterentur. Locato igitur fundamento in Cristo Iesu, ut ait Apostolus, 'Fundamentum positum est, quod est Cristus Iesus', paulatim de vivis et bene sectis et politis lapidibus crescebat edificium, et domus ampliabatur ad suscipiendos pauperes et peregrinos spontaneam adeuntes peregrinacionem et ad Ierusalem celestem festinantes. Sed non defecere[5] temptaciones ini- f. 22ᵛ mici et adversantis hostis insidie, qui plantata eradicare, fundamenta evellere, congregata dispergere, dispersa morti tradere, multiformi dolositate et multimoda calliditate laboravit.

12. *Quomodo Yvonem sibi associavit.* ⟨*Capitulum*⟩ *duodecimum.* Sunt etenim cuncta premissa ex multis pauca que gessit priusquam socium colligeret. Nunc autem plurima restant que per verbum Dei et Spiritus Sancti graciam conservavi.[6] Quodam denique tempore, paululum procedens, vidit quendam[7] virum, nomine Yvonem, mitem et modestum, cui ait, 'Yve, sequere me, et faciam te dispensatorem Domini salvatoris.' Ad quem Yvo, 'Ad te concito, omnibus relictis, veniam.' Huic enim Robertus super singulas elimosinas pauperibus erogandum potestatem prebuit. Sanctus itaque vir, qui novum noviter acceperat, sicut a Deo postulaverat, socium, ne in tanta penitencie asperitate

---

[1] exhauriabat. [2] invenieret. [3] adquiescens et. [4] eligeris.
[5] deficere. [6] conservavit. [7] quondam.

titubaret, verbis huiuscemodi alloquebatur eum et multis ammonicionibus sustentabat, et ne paupertatem abhorreret, multa sanctorum exempla proponebat, volens ut ille paulatim, siccitate estus secularis postposita, hauriret celestis refrigerii et dulcedinis fontem, idem ei promittens quod a veritate promissum est, scilicet, 'Qui bibit ex eo, non sciciet umquam.' Docebat eciam eum quomodo reconsiliari Deo
f. 23 et appropinquare peccator debeat; quibus studiis, quibus laboribus quibusve virtutibus iustus quilibet ad beatorum spirituum consorcium pertineat; quante sit virtutis humilitas astruens qua venitur ad celum; quantaque simplicitas qua penetratur; qualisque sit obediencia qua ad ocultorum Dei noticiam pertingitur; qualis penitencia qua virtus animi possidetur; qualis castitas que proximum facit Deo; qualis virginitas que ambulat cum Cristo; qualis paupertas que regnum[1] celorum possidere facit. Hec et hiis similia vir Deo plenus multociens de die in diem exhortacionis gracia ⟨ad⟩ Yvonem repetebat.

13. *Quomodo Yvo fregit tibiam, et a Roberto est curata. Capitulum decimum tercium.* Hec profecto predicante pastore, lupus invidebat, et qui non potuit pastorem prosternere, ovile insidiando, ovem nititur deglutire. Rapido procul dubio lupus ore ovibus molitur insidias. Insidias vere dixerim quia, ex adverso caulas eorum effodiens, latenter[2] ingreditur, ut, ⟨ut⟩ prius, terrorem excuciat, territo⟨s⟩ malleo caude sue deiciat, deiectos mactet, mactatos postea hyante ore devoret et perdat. Quia vero maior est eius arrogancia quam fortitudo, iste quidem temptator Yvonem aggreditur et multum calamitatum temptacionibus eum instigavit, in tantum quod eum prevalebat. Tunc Yvo, sufferre tam diversarum temptacionum genera exquisita non valens, clam recedere proponebat. Conti⟨n⟩gebat eum per silvam
f. 23v incaute gradientem casu cadere; bene tibia eius ramo cuiusdam arboris fracta, est prostratus fovea. Hoc autem vir Dei in spiritu factum agnoscebat. Unde ad eum, ut prius in omni temptacione sublimandum assolebat, cicius accurrebat. Invenit autem Yvonem pedis dolorem nimium plangentem, et subridendo paululum, 'Ubi est,' ait Yvo, 'hic sermo[3] quem sepius solebas dicere et opere te implere, scilicet te gaudere cum gaudentibus et flere cum flentibus?' Ad quem Robertus ait, 'Rideo plane, quia istud infortunium divina miseracione et dispensacione actum est, et pro emendacione tua et non anime mortificacione. Recordare illius sermonis qui dicit, "Nullus mittens manum ad aratrum et retro respiciens aptus est regno Dei."' Eius autem pedem graviter cruentatum benediccione sue sanctissime manus sanum et incolumem,[4] ut prius, in integrum restauravit, et Yvonem sic sanatum ad cellam suam concito[5] sic reducebat.[6] Sic autem captus est coluber et recessit, scilicet antiqu⟨u⟩s ille et mali-

[1] rignum.   [2] latentur.   [3] (h.s.) hunc sermonem.
[4] incolimem.   [5] concito cui.   [6] raducebat.

Appendix A

gnissimus insidiator tociusque bonitatis et veritatis expers, et cunctorum scelerum adinventor.

14. *Quomodo latrones spoliantes eius cellam interfecti sunt.* ⟨*Capitulum*⟩ *decimum quartum.* Mansit itaque ibidem socius vero suus Yvo, de quo superius mencio facta est, in caritate non ficta indissolubilique amoris vinculo cum Roberto usque ad vite finem in omni tranquilitate et pace et sanctetate proposito. Post hec Yvo discalciatus Eboracum venit, elimosinam pauperibus petiturus, cuius pedum vestigia sanguine tincta et rubricata in gelu et glacie a cunctis agnosci potuerunt. Eodem autem tempore, quinque latrunculi, qui virum Dei in capella Sancte Hylde prius habitantem de pane et caseo et consimilibus spoliaverunt, interfecti sunt ultrice[1] validaque nostri plasmatoris manu. Sic enim subsequitur, ut ait propheta, mors peccatorum pessima. Erat utique in hiis omnibus supra quam dici et credi potest Robertus paciens in vigiliis, sedulus in laboribus spiritualibus, gratus in verbis, graciosus in visu, benignus in simplices, severus contra hostes et malefactores. Ad reficiendum autem nullam preparare, non mensam apponere sibi vir sanctus sinebat. Terra[2] sedes et genua mensa illi multociens erat. Fercula salis condimento condita sunt, et non alio; potus, aqua; panis crude conficitur. Carnes, gustatas nasi odore, omnino commedere respuebat. f. 24

15. *Quomodo mendicavit vaccam, et de fautore.* ⟨*Capitulum*⟩ *decimum quintum.* Si igitur rei veritas et veritatis ordo succedencium adiungitur causis precedentibus,[3] legentibus et audientibus fastidium[4] et derogandi occasionem generare nullatenus debet; quia, etsi quedam[5] tediosa[6] vel quibuscunque emulis superflua videantur, vera tamen et ab hiis qui viderunt et audierunt retexuntur, et[7] pretermitti nequeunt, eo quod alio modo ⟨quam⟩ seriatim res geste[8] nequeunt[9] scire volentibus satisfacere. Non enim pretermittendum est quoddam mirabile quod per eum conditor noster ostendere dignabatur. Quadam vice vir iste modestissimus adivit dominum, ⟨ad⟩ vaccam sibi et egenis penuriam f. 24ᵛ pacientibus protinus postulandam; quam dominus sibi benigne ac libenter annuebat. Habuit enim dominus iste quandam vaccam in foresta sua ferocissimam, quam nullus serviencium appropinquare ausus est. Quam vero dominus, quo animo quave intencione contul⟨er⟩it, ignoro, Roberto ad secum deducendam gratanter assignavit. Pergens quantocius vir Dei Robertus ad forestam, cepit eam in manibus circum collum complexis; quasi agnum mansuetissimum ad domum unde exivit deducere festinavit. Omnibus autem istud miraculum non procul distantibus et iugiter intuentibus et ultra quam credi potest admirantibus, prorumpebat quidam servorum domini in hec verba domino, 'Sciatis[10] me, domine, vaccam Roberto elargitam mihi

---

[1] ultrite. [2] tercia *and* ra *above the line.* [3] precidentibus.
[4] fastigium. [5] quedamque. [6] tediosis. [7] et que.
[8] gesta. [9] negant et. [10] *Read* sinatis?

122 *Appendix A*

ab eo concito optinere.' Cui dominus, 'Ad hoc autem nullum assensum prebeo.' Sed ille quidem fautor, sano consilio[1] domini sui non adquiescens,[2] in veste pauperis, desuper clavata et inveterata, superindutus,[3] pede se finxit claudicare, occulis retro versis ac contractis digitis; Roberto ruit in obviam, voce quoque lugubri multiplicatisque gemitibus et fletibus, sibi et pueris inedia, ut asserebat, depressis erogari flebiliter postulavit. Quam vir Cristi, licet actus subtilitatis agnovit in spiritu, benigne tribuebat, dicens, 'Deus dedit et Deus habebit; sed tibi continget quod fingere presumpsisti.' Cumque fautor iste cum vacca decedere attemptasset, immobilis permanebat et, cum procedere vellet, ex facto claudicavit. Et cum percepisset divinam
f. 25 vindicacionem super se evenisse eo quod virum Dei deludebat, dimissa vacca, clamavit post tergum Roberti dicens, 'O vir Dei, mihi de iniuria tibi illata clementer indulgere digneris.' Cui vir strenuus modeste ac benigne indulgebat; et homo, sanitati pristine restitutus, cum gaudio ac leticia ad propria remeavit.

16. *De cervis in segite eius captis et inclusis. Capitulum decimum sextum.* Magnificavit autem Dominus electum suum Robertum crebris et inauditis miraculorum signis et de die in diem nomen sanctitatis eius ac famam ampliavit ac nobilitavit, addens magna maioribus, miraculis succedentibus, ut esset universis cohabitantibus spectaculum sanctitatis ac informacio omnium bonorum miris operibus que per eum Dominus ostendere est dignatus. Choruscavit enim multis miraculis, que pro multitudine ac temporis brevitate et prolixitate historie nequeunt enarrari. Sed inter cetera unum preterire nolo, quod de cervis de foresta sepius segetes viri Dei invadentibus, conculcantibus et consumentibus, adivit dominum, de dampnis sibi per cervos illatis corditer conquerendo et deprecando ut eorum tutam custodiam adhiberet. Cui dominus, 'Tibi plenam facultatem, o Roberte, tribuo ut hos in horrio tuo includere valeas donec tibi de dampnis constiterit plenissime satisfactum.' Exivit autem homo Dei in agrum et cervos captos in segite coram eo, motu virge, ut agnos
f. 25v mansuetissimos[4] fugavit, ac in horrio suo, ut iusticia exigit, tutissime includebat. Deinde Robertus regressus domino factum insinuavit, precipiens nichilominus ut eos a clausura sua reducere festinaret. Quod videns dominus et ultra quam credi potest admirans intra se, dicebat, 'Tibi concedo et libere possidendos tribuo captos cervos in segete et ad inponendos aratro sive in consimilibus quibuscunque aliis operibus agriculture, prout melius et commodius tibi videris,[5] expedire.' Cui gracias exhibens, ad cellam est reversus. Quid plura? Cervos horrio reducebat et in aratro suo coniunctim copulavit, et per singulos dies ad terram suam excolendam more bovino coegit attractare. Pretactum miraculum viderunt qui tunc temporis aderant et

[1] concilio.   [2] adquiescens se.   [3] superindutus et.
[4] (a.m.) agni mansuetissimi.   [5] videns.

quidam qui successerunt. Sed et succedentes amplius videbunt, quia, teste veritate, qui credit, opera que facit et ipse faciet et maiora horum faciet; et alibi, 'Si credideritis, maius hiis videbitis.'

17. *Quomodo Sathanas eidem apparuit in precibus pernoctanti.* ⟨*Capitulum*⟩ *decimum septimum.* Quadam autem nocte, cum vir Domini Robertus proposuisset totam sequentem noctem insompnem ducere et adorando Deum rogare ut ipse, qui est dator recti consilii[1] et bonorum operum adiutor, secundum beneplacitum voluntatis sue consilium[2] dirigeret et propositum adiuvaret, et[3] sic in oracione pernoctasset, summo diluculo, paulatim maxillam manu sustentam pavimento declinans dormitavit. Et ecce adversarius, iniquitatis tocius auctor, affuit, sperans aliquid se facere per ipsum, cum nichil prius in membris suis, per quos adversus eum molitus fuerat, potuisset, in subsannando et insultando loquens, 'Eya![4] eya! multa proposuisti, sed ad quem finem devenire[5] speras, qui nec in unius noctis proposito perseverare potuisti?' Tunc demon ille omnia vasa Dei viri, pulmenta, panem et consimilia turpissimis manibus tangere presumebat. Cui vir Dei ait, 'Egredere, miser, egredere, et me tuis fraudulenciis non obtemperantem ulterius non presumas inquietare.' Taliter ergo spiritus malignus confusus ab eo recedebat. Omnium ergo destitutus subsidio, Domino tantum fultus[6] auxilio, oracionibus et psalmodiis iugiter incumbebat. Vanitati et voluptati secularium contrarius prorsus existens, contemplacioni intendebat.

18. *Quomodo aqua benedicta eundem demonem effugavit.* ⟨*Capitulum*⟩ *decimum octavum.* Huic autem falso et maligno spiritui non sufficit, nec miratur si absorbeat mare, sed eciam Iordanem totum sorbere nititur; qui manifeste ad integrum seducere non potuit, iterum, occulciores presumptuose sumens insidias, redire non metuebat. Alio quoque tempore, idem artificio⟨s⟩us decepcionis aliud genus exquirebat. Apparuit namque in effigie unius nigerimi rustici, fuligini⟨bu⟩s turpioris, stridentibus dentibus; Roberto se opposuit et eum ab inceptis oracionibus impedire conabatur. Sed vir sanctus eius insidias, quas frequencius sustinebat, minime formidans, arrepto aspersorio, proiecit aquam benedictam super demonem sibi insultantem. Quam nequaquam ferens, cum impetu exiliit ab oratorio, fetidum post se odorem dereliquit.[7] Tunc Robertus, 'O miser et infelix et omnibus creaturis deterior, tu, inquam, qui signaculum similitudinis Dei fuisti et superbiendo veritatis huius cognicionem perdidisti et sic in tua pertinacia perseverans dampnacionis eterne sentenciam mereberis introire!'

19. *Quomodo demon*[8] *cellam eius incendere attemptavit.* ⟨*Capitulum*⟩ *decimum nonum.* Verumptamen de adversario interim pretermittendum non est quod viro Dei, sicut sepius, aggredi et insultari occurrebat.

---

[1] concilii.   [2] concilium.   [3] ut.   [4] exa.
[5] devenrie.   [6] stultus.   [7] dereliquid.   [8] demodo.

Apparuit enim Roberto preces continuanti, flexis genibus, in effigie pueri duodecim annorum, ut chachinnis et ingenti strepitu a fructu deprecacionum impediret. Sed virum Dei in precibus perseverantem videns quod impedire non valebat, omne stramentum capellule sue in unum collectum in igne deiecit, ut sic domum concremare niteretur. Sed crucis signaculo facto, ut vapor fumi ad nichilum est redactum. Alio quoque tempore, Sathanas in specie pueri sexdecim annorum se transformavit ut Robertum terreret, sed non prevaluit quia eum virga cedebat, ut sepius facere consuevit, et sic flagellatum deiecit. Et sic inmundus spiritus, nullas paciens moras, fetentissime urine feda relinquens vestigia, aufugit. Plura quoque tentamentorum genera antiqui serpentis calliditate exquisita passus est, que seriatim pro multitudine eorum in codicibus inserere nequimus; que⟨m⟩ procul dubio electus Dei Robertus divinitus a sua cellula procull abiecit et abire coegit.

20. *Quomodo Iohannes rex illustrissimus Robertum visitavit.* ⟨*Capi-*
f. 27 *tulum*⟩ *vicesimum.* Quoniam igitur divinis omnino mancipatus obsequiis quasi pro nichilo celestium respectu reputabat secularia cuncta, sic ei fere per omnia Domino favorem et graciam incipiente, ad vota successit ut summo regi in nullo defuerit et terreno principi in suis agendis nusquam defecerit, tanquam Deo[1] rectore sic actus suos librans ac moderans, ut ordine conpetenti semper divina preponens, que Cesaris erant Cesari et que Dei Deo.[2] Igitur ut aliqua ex hiis generaliter dicta sunt, specialiter dicantur. Audita fama huius viri et in patriis divulgata, illustris rex Iohannes, precibus domini Briani rogatus, ad cellam Roberti cum comitibus suis humiliter descendebat. Ingressi autem capellulam, virum Dei coram altari in oracionibus prostratum reperierunt, qui vero pro nimio strepitu ingrediencium ab incepta oracione desistere nolebat, quanquam[3] in spiritu agnosceret regis sui adventum gloriosum. Videns autem Brianus quod regi non assurgebat nec ei debitam reverenciam exhibebat, ait, 'Frater Roberte, surge velociter. Ecce presens est dominus noster rex Iohannes.' Qui continuo surgens, ait ad Brianum, 'Indica mihi quis istorum est rex meus.' Cui Brianus, 'Iste est rex meus Iohannes, regum illustrissimus.' Tunc vir Domini, arrepta quadam spica, quam in palma porri-
f. 27ᵛ gebat regi, sic inquiens, 'Potesne, domine mi rex, tale tua virtute ex nichilo creare ?' Tunc quidam de astantibus dixerunt, 'Hic homo insani capitis est, et fatuum factis evidentibus se apertissime fatetur.' Ad quos quidam sic responderunt, 'Nequaquam, sed hic Dei famulus sapiens est et prudens, quia eum interius habet[4] inhabitantem Spiritum Sanctum, in quo continetur omnis sapiencia divinitatis.' Videns autem rex Domini electum cultoremque Trinitatis, proprio stimulatus animo, ait, 'Pete, Roberte,[5] de me quicquid tibi necesse

[1] Deoque. [2] *Verb omitted here or after* preponens. [3] quam enim.
[4] habet per. [5] Roberter.

Appendix A

fuerit, et postulata queque dare tibi non differam.' Robertus respondit, 'Omnia mihi bona transitoria habundant et pecunie non indigeo. Nichil enim christiano ambi.endum[1] est preter Cristum.' Tunc exivit rex cum suis et ad propria declinavit. Audito ab Yvone quod elimosinas pauperibus a rege non postulasset, obiurgavit Robertum, sibi imponendo crimen captivitatis eo quod noluit prece pia apud regem pauperibus subvenire. Quare[2] Robertus regi reversus, ait, 'Memento, domine mi rex, quod mortalis es et peccata elimosinis piis redimere deberes. Unde caritative pauperibus et egenis meis elimosinam erogare digneris.' Respondens autem rex ait, 'Ego de vicin⟨i⟩ore nemore meo, quantum potes una caruca in agricultura⟨m⟩ redigere, tibi tribuo in perpetuam elimosinam.' O virum singularis gracie munere pollentem, et[3] tremendis tirannis cunctisque terribilem, coram quo principes loqui cessabant! Nec propriam fragilitatem attendebat sive inpotenciam; intrepida voce Iohannem monebat, regem reverendum. f. 28

21. *Quomodo rector de Knaresburgo decimas vendicavit.* ⟨*Capitulum*⟩ *vicesimum primum.* Mira Dei virtus, et mira viri Dei gracia, quod principis animus Willelmi de Scutivilla et consilium, qui tam effrenis et efferus fuit, necnon et paulo ante graviter offensus in ipso viri graciosi adventu, incontinenti mitescere⟨t⟩, quod statim ipsum Willelmum in osculo susceperit[4] et digno debitoque cum honore tractaverit et elimosina⟨m⟩ munifice erogaverit. Inter cetera a⟨u⟩tem huius Deo dicati viri insignia, unum occurrit memorie, quod preterire renuo. Cumque totam terram arrabilem, quam ex donis et concessionibus magnatum vir Dei ad usus pauperum excoluisset, seminasset et ad maturos fructus protulisset, prostravisset et ad orrium suum inducere proposuisset, occurrit rector ecclesie Knaresburgensis cum magno impetu decimas de eis petiturus. Cui Robertus subnititur, dicens nequaquam se de novis assertis sive de novalibus et de elimosinis pauperum debere[5] decimare. 'Animadvertite,' inquit, 'qualiter hic iurisperitus, immo iure perditus, donum Deo plus diligens, pecuniam pietati preferens, nummum minime anteponens, de frugibus meis decimas, suadente diabolo, exigere presumit.' Rector ait Roberto, 'Tu, Roberte, velis nolis, mihi decimas prestabis.' Ad quem Robertus, 'Tu a me decimas violenter exigis; ego autem tibi do malediccionem f. 28ᵛ Dei et pauperum eius, quorum bona sibi pro sustentacione eorundem caritative erogantur, que ab eis iam rapere non pertimescis; legista enim, corrige[6] te, lingue tue lanista.' ⟨Im⟩modicum illud membrum, quo eggregium Dei virum frequenter offendebat, Deo vindicante, horribiliter dilaniavit. Rector vero, dum aliena bona sibi appropriare ac usurpare nititur, e mundo egressurus nec sua distribuere est iusto Dei iudicio permissus. Sic utique iste devotissimus Dei famulus in sanctitate proficiens, perturbatores et cismaticos omnes persequens

---

[1] *Read* ambigendum?   [2] quainre.   [3] qui.
[4] susceperet.   [5] deberet.   [6] corrigi.

Appendix A

et detestans, bonos amplectens, desolatis dans consilium,[1] pauperes, orphanos et viduas sustentans, seipsum tam minoribus quam maioribus affabilem exhibens, divine largitatis et gracie non in . . . or,[2] Domino Deo suo per singulos dies bone opinionis et intime suavitatis et dulcedinis offerebat consciencia⟨m⟩ (?).

22. *Quomodo prophetavit Robertus, Bryano mortem predicendo et de Fontinensibus.* ⟨*Capitulum*⟩ *vicesimum secundum.* O quanta Dei pietas, bonitas et gracia, quantaque descendens in terram deorsum celestis gracia, tam pio benignitatis studio temporis malicie remedia prestans, quod in hiis ultimis diebus, quibus mundi tam caritas frigescit quam etas per sanctorum quorundam merita simul et exempla fides gelidior excitatur et inflammatur, per hec eadem suffragia indeficiones caritas[3] lampas accendatur. De signis, virtutibus, meritis et miraculis quibusdam, que gloriose Dominus noster propter honorem nostri

f. 29 patroni Roberti eggregii operari est dignatus, nunc divina opitulante clemencia planis admodum verbis et non polito stilo[4] explicare curavi et curabo prout primitus. Inter multa quoque gesta nostri patroni laudabilia et cunctis collata beneficia ac preconia, silendum esse non censui quomodo salvator, qui in sanctis suis semper est mirabilis, sanctum suum prophetico illustravit spiritu. Brianus vero, de quo superius mencionem fecimus, mandato domini regis pro certis rebus et causis regnum concernentibus sive expediendum[5] ad australes partes missus, extitit. Ob quam causam prosperandam, ad Robertum reversus, munus sue virtuose benediccionis et allocucionis humiliter expetivit, et se suis devotis precibus intime commendavit. Cui data benediccione iste vir strenuus prophetice est proloquutus,[6] 'Ibis enim cum tuis ad destinata loca cum pace et tranquillitate, et omnes actus tui prosperabuntur, ad propria minime reversurus.' Tristis exiens, et secundum viri Dei vaticinium omnia sibi evenerunt. Ibidem autem aliquandiu moram faciens, bonis operibus et elimosinis plenus, in pace quievit. Hoc eciam inter cetera notabile censui quod idem vir perfectissimus ante obitum suum prophetavit, dicens, quod monachi Fontanensis cenobii magna cum instancia ruerent ac instarent, egressa anima, corpus exanime de hoc habitaculo deportare secum

f. 29ᵛ in monasterio suo humando[7] cum honore. Quibus precepit brachio seculari resistere eciam, si necesse fuerit, volens ut ubi corpus ultimum exaltaret[8] spiritum, ibidem corpus perpetuo remaneret. Quod et factum est. Magne denique debilitatis erat vir strenuus in suo corpore, utpote longa et gravi attritus asperitate penitencie, sed multo amplius crevit infirmitas cum labor itinerancium et domestice cure sollicitudo ac mutacio diversorum dierum et inquietudinis assiduitas.[9]

[1] concilium.   [2] *Read* immemor?   [3] (i.c.) *Read* in defectiones caritatis?   [4] (p.s.) politus stilus.   [5] (s.e.) *Read* ibi expediendis?   [6] preloquutus.   [7] *Read* humandum?   [8] *Read* exhalaret?   [9] *Verb omitted.*

Appendix A

Cuncta autem que per eum Dominus operari dignatus est, non est possibile alicui soli narrare, nec alicui soli possibile fuit scire vel cognoscere.

23. *Quomodo Robertus morti appropinquavit.* ⟨*Capitulum*⟩ *vicesimum tercium.* Cum igitur hiis et similibus moribus et actibus vir sanctus in terra se perornaret ac venustaret, in brevi rapiendus e medio ne posset deterius forte mutari, graviter infirmatus ac egritudine exagitatus, demum, gravescente morbo, cum diem novissimum sibi videret imminere, iussit sibi viaticum afferri, parans interim lampadem suam, ut, veniente Domino, posset ei prudenter occurrere. Porro quam preclaram lampadem, quam preciosum oleum penes se haberet reconditum, testantur ipsa verba evangelii. Audientes autem Fontanenses monachi de transitu huius viri gloriosi, cum habitu suo festinantes venerunt, in quo corpus involvi ac sepeliri deberet. Quibus vir Dei ait, 'Sufficit mihi vestis propria, nec aliam concupisco.' Appropinquante illo morti, Yvo cum ceteris lacrimabiliter ait, 'Nobis, pater, petimus, tue benediccionis munus impende.' Ac hos ilico benedixit. Nec mora, morbo urgencius invalescente, vir sanctitate conspicuus, rebus humanis exemptus, feliciter ab hac vita migravit ad Dominum. Tunc Yvo cum astantibus lugubres voces cum crebris singultibus emittentes, dixerunt, 'Heu! heu! ad quem in tribulacionibus et pressuris constituti ibimus?' Defuncto itaque beate et digne memorie patre nostro Roberto, advocato et patrono, spirituque suo ad summe felicitatis eternitatem vocato, sanctoque corpore ipsius exanimi relicto, idem cum omni diligencia preparavit ad humandum. f. 30

24. *Quomodo Fontinenses irruebant pro corpore capiendo.* ⟨*Capitulum*⟩ *vicesimum quartum.* Cum autem corpus patroni nostri benignissimi omni quo decuit honore conditum fuisset, et huiusmodi fama in patria divulgata[1] fuisset,[2] iterum occurrerunt Fontanenses et eum habitu suo induerunt,[3] quod, eo vivente, facere permissi[4] non fuerunt. Insuper, secundum propheciam viri Dei, Fontanenses corpus rapere et secum in monasterio humando[5] vi et armis studuerunt. Sed illis utique multitudo non minima castri Knaresburgensis restitit armatorum. Dicebantt enim Fontanenses quod magis conveniens esset ac decencius corpus talis eggregii viri in sollempniori loco humari quam in loco sterili et fere ex toto desolato. Alii autem denegabant,[6] dicentes quod precipue cum adhuc vivens homo precepisset et usque sue hoc f. 30ᵛ voluntatis devocio postulans demonstrasset quod inter fratres suos et filios, quos Deo et Dei verbo pauperitatis sue tempore genuerat, sepeliri et requiescere debuisset. Hec erat contencio et evidens utrimque[7] proponebatur certeque racionis responsio. Tandem autem Fontanenses tristes ad propria sunt reversi. Expletis autem funeralibus

[1] duvulgata.   [2] fuerat.   [3] induerunt per.   [4] promissi.
[5] *Read* humare?   [6] denegabant.   [7] utrumque.

Appendix A

omnibus, cum honore summo corpus deferunt in capella Sancte Crucis, quam frater eius Walterus sibi construxerat, tumulandum scilicet coram altari in sarchofago,[1] in quo nondum quisquam antea positus fuerat, ubi, in tumulo[2] diligenter spertinintate (?)[3] adornato, diem exspectat novissimum in spe certe resurreccionis et gloria.

25. *De exequiis Roberti et post mortem miraculis.* ⟨*Capitulum*⟩ *vicesimum quintum.* Convenerunt utique ad eius exequias celebrandas solempniter conventicula non modica egenorum, divitum et pauperum, necnon agmina religiosorum, utriusque sexus populus, non mediocriter dolentes quod tam sanctissimi privarent⟨ur⟩ pastoris presencia, qui tam frequenter eos in omni tribulacione solebat consolari, sed pocius congaudentes quod ad superna tenderet pro eis Dominum perpetuo rogaturus precis patrociniis. Quis autem exprimere posset quanta[4] virorum et mulierum ad corpus, in capella iam positum, catervatim accedencium et feretrum osculancium, et ad corpus sacrum ac laudabili presumpcione pariter et devocione, nondum tumulatum, nondum signis et miraculis clarificatum aut canonicatum, aurumque et argentum offerencium multitudo currunt; unde et tanta tamque conferta[5] utriusque sexus hominum ad hec in ipsa capellula turba confluxit, quod vix[6] infra et extra loci ambitus compressi stare non valebant. Ad cuius gloriosam tumbam singulis afflictis sive in aliqua egritudine depressis, precibus huius sancti viri refugium est eis celitus inpensum, Domino sanctum suum diversorum miraculorum signis magnificante, prout scripturis et pictis figuris circa tumbam dependentibus poterit unusquisque evidenter oculis aspicere. Post eius autem obitum inauditis cepit iste inclitus Domini confessor Robertus choruscare miraculis, cecis visum, claudis gressum, surdis auditum, loquelam mutis restituens. Deinde leprosos mundans, consolidans paraliticos, ydropisim et omnia membrorum[7] incurabilium genera curans, resuscitans mortuos, demonibus eciam et elementis omnibus mirabiliter imperans, ad inusitata quoque et inaudita signa potencie sue manum extendebat. Unde clerici plurimi laici⟨que⟩, Deum publice laudantes, vocibus ac votis huiuscemodi preconia Deique magnalia prorumpentes, 'Mirabilis Deus in sanctis suis et magnus in operibus suis'; item, 'Magnus Dominus et laudabilis nimis, et magnitudinis eius non est finis, quique, de fine in finem attingens fortiter et disponens omnia suaviter, vivit et vincit, regnat et imperat in secula seculorum. Amen.'

[1] sarchofogo.　[2] timulo.　[3] *Read* supra trinitate?
[4] quanto.　[5] conserta.　[6] (q.v.) *Read* qui vi?　[7] *Read* morborum?

APPENDIX B

The following Latin prose life of St Robert is contained in the British Museum Manuscript, Harley 3775, ff. 74^r–77^r. Ff. 74^r–76^v are in a fourteenth-century hand, and f. 77^r is in a hand of c. 1400.[1] MS. Harley 3775, which is a composite manuscript, is defective in places, so that parts of the life of St. Robert are missing. The text which appears below omits those lines in § 1 which have no bearing on *M*.

1. . . . Aperiens igitur os suum, a patre sancti viri, qui Toccus f. 74 Flos nuncupabatur, et matre eius Sunniva, qualiter sub lege degentes coniugali ambo Deum timerent[2] et de sua substancia honorarent, manus largas extendendo pauperibus, narracionem texere cepit subscriptam . . . .

2. ⟨B⟩eatus[3] igitur Robertus ad gloriam patrie predestinatus superne, advesperascente iam mundo, mortalibus in quos fines seculi devenerunt, in hoc caliginoso errantibus exilio tanquam sidus nove claritatis viam iusticie sue conversacionis . . . .[4]

3. . . . ceperat, monasterium relinquens ad propria reversus est. f. 75 Hinc nonnulli, solo nomine religiosi, sibi placentes et de specie sanctitatis singulariter gloriantes, qui oculos nucis[5] habuerunt, ut in oculis alienis festucam clare viderent; quorum erat studium detestandum meliorem vitam dente carpere canino, aliorum profectui invidere,[6] aliene perfectioni derogare, Dei famulum ordinis fugitivum apostatamque appellabant. O execrabile Phariseorum fermentum, quod est ypocrisis! ut enim maiorem ab hominibus sibi vendicarent favorem, quasi sub pretextu vere religionis, coram populo Dei servo detrahere non desistebant. At miles Cristi, supra firmam petram fundatus, a verbis impiorum non timuit nec iaculis conviciorum[7] cessit, set indutus lorica iusticie, scuto protectus paciencie, per infam⟨i⟩am et bonam famam cum apostolo surda aure transivit.[8]

4. ⟨I⟩nterea[9] cum in domo paterna per dies aliquod moraretur, anxius ad superna suspirans, quorumdam didicit relacione virum quemdam heremiticam vitam ducentem non longe a villa que Knaresburgus appellatur, sub rupe latere. Erat quidem vir ille miles famosus et dives operum (?); ut iram regis Ricardi, ob quandam offensam eius animam querentis, ad tempus declinaret, in habitu heremitico, ne a satellitibus regis agnosceretur, latitare decrevit. Instinctu igitur illius cuius moderamine universa reguntur, parentibus eius inconsultis, urbem occulte relinquens ad militem prenotatum ardenti

---

[1] *Dated by Dr. Cyril Wright.* [2] tenuereret. [3] *Space left for initial capital.* [4] *One folio missing between f. 74 and f. 75.* [5] *Read* noctis? [6] invudere. [7] convisciorum. [8] *In margin in hand 2:* De primo eius adventu ad heremum de Knarsburgho. [9] *Space left for initial capital.*

130   Appendix B

animo vir Dei devotus confugit. De cuius adventu plurimum ille gavisus gracias egit omnipotenti, qui ad suum socatium (?) collegam ei transmisit ingenuum. Habitaverunt itaque simul in loco horroris et vaste solitudinis donec rex Ricardus, lege mortis compellente, viam universe carnis ingrediens, mundo valefaceret. Rege igitur de medio sublato, memoratus miles non Cristi set mundi, qui putabatur ad aratrum Dei manum misisse, respiciens retro, ad uxorem et filios, ut canis ad vomitum, reversus est.[1]

5. ⟨P⟩ost[2] fugam vero militis ignavi, miles Cristi humano destitutus solacio, sedere solitarius et tacere nondum didicerat. Unde ad quandam matronam nobilem, Helenam nomine, in partibus illis habitantem, eis elemosinas conferrendo suffragium petiturus humiliter accessit. Quem mulier pietate plena tanquam angelum Dei vultu f. 75ᵛ suscipiens gratulabundo, dedit ei ecclesiam Sancte Hilde in saltu de Knaresburgo constructam, ubi quondam villa grandis que Rothferlingtoun vocabatur a rege Stephano subversa refertur. De terra autem adiacente quantum ei fodere placuit concessit, et victui necessaria liberaliter impendit. Habitavit igitur in loco memorato, semotus a conturbacione hominum, fere per annum, carnem suam continua penitencia affligens, et cum viciis et concupisce⟨n⟩ciis crucifigens. Quod videns ille, cuius invidia mors introivit in orbem terrarum, ad infestandum Dei famulum sua excitavit membra,[3] latrunculos scilicet, qui illum supra inquietarent, ad eius cellam veniendo et pauperum alimenta diripiendo. Conturbatum est igitur cor eius intra se, ita ut vivere tederet a pio desiderio fraudatum. Quesierat enim pectoris pacem et ecce turbacio, illo procurante qui eum ab arce sancte conversacionis nitebatur deicere. Tandem memor illius evangelii: 'Si vos persecuti fuerint in una civitate, fugite in aliam,' relicto latronum latibulo, ad matronam superius memoratam revertebatur, mala que a ministris Sathane frequenter pertulerat[4] illi per ordinem exponens. At illa eius condolens angustie et affliccioni pie compaciens, cum comperisset quod sub pariete ecclesie de Spoford manere et Deo vacare desideraret, votis illius clementer inclinata, postulacioni servi Dei illico prebuit assensum, eius inopiam ex sua habundancia, prout pridem consueverat, temperare non desistens. Cumque dulcedine superne patrie iugiter intentus ibidem per dimidium annum moram fecisset, cepit multitudo plebis circum⟨i⟩acentis patrie ad eum catervatim confluere et tanquam sanctum venerari. Attendens igitur vir Deo plenus rebus secundis multo plures in retroactis seculis seductos quam adversitatibus superatos, favorem transitorium populorumque frequenciam declinare proposuit. Inter duo denique pericula constitutus, anime scilicet,[5] si illic moram faceret diuturnam, et substancie,

[1] *In margin in hand 2*: De mora eius fere per annum in foresta.
[2] *Space left for initial capital.*   [3] menbra.   [4] pretulerat.
[5] sciliceet.

Appendix B 131

si locum peteret priorem, elegit pocius sua visibilibus exponere predonibus, quam invisibilium hostium ruinam anime querentium circumveniri[1] astuciis. Noverat siquidem quod species mulieris multos decepit. Igitur timens ne forte[2] oculus depredaretur animam illius si in medio mulierum diucius commoraretur, cum beato Iob pepigit fedus cum oculis suis ne cogitaret quidem de virgine. Et quia non expedit intueri quod licite non potest concupisci, de medio incendii antequam ureretur saluberrimum fore fugere decrevit, precavens f. 76 eciam ne de verbo ocioso in extremo accusaretur examine, turbarum tumultuancium cohabitacionem vitando, digitum ori suo cogitavit imponere. Sciebat quippe in multiloquio peccatum non deesse.[3] Dum hec itaque animo revolveret gemebundo et qualiter desiderium suum perduceret ad effectum penitus ignoraret, monachi de monasterio Sancte Trinitatis Eboracensis civitatis apud Hedlay[4] commorantes omnem ei se exibituros spoponderunt humanitatem, si eorum copularetur collegio; quod audiens athleta Cristi semper invictus, talibus fidem adhibens promissis, ad locum eorum celere[5] gressum declinavit. More igitur consueto semetipsum ibidem celestibus extenuans disciplinis, accinxit fortitudine lumbos suos, omnem voluptatem et carnis petulanciam viriliter coartando, et roboravit brachium suum armis penitencie, contra principatus et potestates tenebrarum harum indefessis viribus pugnaturus. Videntes itaque monachi quod illorum conversacionem viri Dei perfectio longe transcenderet, livoris facibus mox inflammati, oderant eum nec poterant ei quicquam pacifice loqui. Unde et dixerunt: 'Gravis est nobis ad videndum homo iste singularis, quia contrarius est operibus nostris et nobis in habitu et victu omnino dissimilis.'[6] Erat autem eius indumentum una tantum alba cuculla vetusta, desuper panniculis undique consuta, que pocius nuditatem utcumque excluderet quam vitalem corpori calorem conferret. Discalciatus[7] eciam usque ad extrema vite sue tempora semper pergebat. Alimenta quidem, quibus apustus (?) nimis maceratus ieiuniis qualitercumque sustentavit, erant tantum panis et olera. Panis vero non de adipe frumenti sed de quatuor partibus farine ordeacie et quinta cineris cribrati proporcionaliter commixtis conficiebatur. Pulmenta quidem, a pulmentis Esau de venacione delicatis multum distancia, erant de marcidis olerum foliis sub fabarum modica sine sale minuta[8] ordei farinula.[9] Et ut omnem[10] gutturi delectabilem adimeret saporem, pulmento semel cocto per septimane circulum solebat esse contentus. Quod quidem spacium tot dierum ita acidum reddiderat et insipidum, ut de eo si quis modicum degustaret, cum filiis prophetarum olim sub Elyseo conversancium: 'Mors in olla, vir Dei!' protinus conclamaret. Nullum denique edulium de creaturis quas anima movit sensitiva

---

[1] circumveni. [2] ne forte *twice*. [3] *In margin in hand 2:* De conversacione eius apud Hedlay. [4] Heldlay. [5] celeri. [6] dissimulis. [7] Discalcinatus. [8] minita. [9] farunula. [10] omne.

132 Appendix B

confectum voluit ore contingere. Huic igitur fideli quem Dominus pane lacrimarum cibaverat et de fonte voluntatis sue suaviter potaverat, immo ebriaverat, cuius conversacio iam in celis erat, que quondam tangere[1] nolebat anima eius pre amaritudine, tanquam paradysi delicie placuerunt. O mira viri Dei solicitudo circa cordis custodiam! Nam ut thesaurum in vase fictili contentum securius conservaret, vas illud afflictionis igne extra modum non cessabat solidare.[2]

f. 76ᵛ 6. ⟨C⟩uius[3] rei causa se monachis displicere patenter addiscens, maxime quia illis in moribus renuit conformari, ad ecclesiam Sancte Hilde, quam prius deseruerat, assensu matrone prenotate iterum requisito, redire proposuit, malens cum feris et furibus quam cum fratribus malignantibus commorari. Mulier igitur clarissima, clementer illius ... orta,[4] manum suam inopi aperire non distulit. Mox etenim de terra circumiacente[5] quantum scelere (?) una potuit carruca, deieluit (?), eidem duos boves cum vacca et equo in subsidium[6] agri colendi iungendo. Vicini etiam, Deum timentes et servum eius, de suis facultatibus pari devocione sustentare volentes illi tot an.ma[7] agriculture[8] necessaria protinus contulerunt.[9] Edificavit igitur ibi, nobili matrona manum porrigente adiutricem,[10] habitaculum in quo tam transeuntes quam ei famulantes congrue reciperentur.[11] Constructo etiam postmodum horeo[12] in quo fruges reconderentur, vir Deo deditus, cui scurilitates et stultiloquia[13] semper erant inimica, suorum vaniloquia devitans, in ecclesia cibum sumere et in oracionibus[14] pernoc⟨t⟩are consuevit. Quatuor quippe habens famulos eorum tali modo ordinavit officia[15]—duos quidem agriculture deputavit, tercium necessariis domi preparandis, quartum ser⟨v⟩um per provinciam habuit occupatum in elemosinis colligendis quas erogaret egenis.[16]

7. ⟨D⟩olens[17] igitur hostis generis humani, machinamentis eius prioribus[18] iam irritatis, adversum Cristi militem nondum se prevaluisse, adversarium ei crudelissimum, Domino permittente, suscitavit. Eo namque tempore vir nobilis et baronum famosissimus in Anglia, Willelmus de Stutewille, cum venandi gracia saltus loca ibidem lustrasset opaca, contigit ut per servi Dei transiret habitacula. Elevatis itaque oculis, cum edificia cerneret de novo constructa, et nonnullis referentibus quemdam sancte conversacionis habitare heremitam cognovisset, totus incanduit ira illumque simulatorem ac latronum fautorem indignanti voce appellans, iuravit per oculos Dei

---

[1] tangerer. [2] *In margin in hand 2*: De regressione eius ad ecclesiam Sancte Hilde. [3] *Space left for initial capital.* [4] *Difficult to read.*
[5] ornicacente. [6] supersidium. [7] *Difficult to read.*
[8] agricilture. [9] contuleit. [10] adiutrucem. [11] recipientur.
[12] horee. [13] stultuloquia. [14] oraccibus. [15] efficia.
[16] *In margin in hand 2*: Qualiter Willelmus de Stutevilla persecutus est eum. [17] *Space left for initial capital.* [18] prior ibi.

Appendix B

—tali quidem iuracioni assuescebat os eius—quod in suo nemore ulterius non habitaret. Convocatis igitur absque mora qui eum sequebantur satellitibus, iussit ut habitatore protinus expulso, domos eius demolerentur et subverterent. Adiecit insuper et hec: 'Si' inquid, 'seductor ille callidus, qui mentes simplicium suis immutat prestigiis[1] et alienat, de isto loco iuxta preceptum meum egredi contempserit, cum universis ad eum pertinentibus vivum illum incendite.' At illi, subt⟨r⟩acta de loco domini sui presencia, Altissimum metuentes et ob hoc eius famulo defferentes, indiscreta imperia opere adimplere discrete dissimulabant. Verum, quoniam multe tribulaciones iustorum et omnes qui pie vivere volunt persecucionem pacientur, ut huic iusto temptacio minime deesset, Domino volente accidit ut peragratis saltus angulis in quibus erat ferarum maior copia, ad cellam f. 77 servi Dei vir prenotatus leone ferocior iterum diverteret. Cumque vidisset sua imperia ad effectum nondum perducta, dentibus suis fremens, gravi interposito sacramento, suis comminabatur subiectis eorum oculos fore eruendos si quod superius preceperat perficere deferrent. Qui sevientis domini sui manus timentes ultrices, omnia servi Dei habitacula, licet inviti, diruerunt et terre funditus coequaverunt. Unde versa est in luctum cithera eius et organum eius in vocem flencium. Terrores enim Dei contra eum militabant, cuius sagitte in eo erant infixe. Potuit quidem ea hora, cum sancto Iob facultatibus caducis spoliato et super modum afflicto, premissa gemendo recitare et que secuntur conquirendo[2] subiungere: 'Mutatus es mihi, Domine, in crudelem et in duricia manus tua[3] adversaria mihi; set licet affligens me dolore non parcas, iustificationem meam quam cepi tenere, te assistente, nunquam deseram, adversitate fractus vel quavis temptacione pulsatus.' Et quia iustum non contristavit quicquid ei accidit, Domino fortitudinem et constantiam prestante,[4] in voces prorupit consimiles: 'Dominus mihi adiutor, non timebo quid faciat mihi homo. Iudicabit enim nocentes me et expugnabit impugnantes mihi. Illi quidem derelictus sum iam pauper, qui est adiutor in oportunitatibus, in tribulatione.' Conversusque ad eos qui eius domata in terram detraxerant, confidenter ait: 'Revertimini et renunciate domino vestro, qui confidit in virtute sua et in multitudine diviciarum suarum gloriatur, prevalens in vanitate sua, cuius superbia et indignacio plus quam eius fortitudo, quem castrum muro inexpugnabili cum propugnaculis vallatum recipit et, ut creditur, ab omni hoste reddit securum, quod, velit nolit, non procul a suo castello castra mea, immo Dei excelsi, in proximo sum metaturus, et tabernacula in seculum permansura iuxta turrem eius fixurus.'

[1] prestidiis. [2] conquirundo. [3] tue. [4] prerante (?).

APPENDIX C

The following Latin verse life of St. Robert (*LVL*.) is contained in the British Museum Manuscript, Egerton 3143, ff. 1ʳ–7ᵛ.

f. 1   De nobilitate vite Sancti Roberti confess(oris)

    In excelsis salvatori,   1
    Patri, proli⟨s⟩ plasmatori,
    Paradisi possessori,
      Deus, desiderium,
    Hymp⟨n⟩us, honor ac honestas,   2
    Principatus et potestas,
    Qui emundat mentes mestas,
      Sint, simul imperium.
    Postquam cun⟨c⟩ta inchoavit,   3
    Prothoplaustum procreavit.
    Proth dolor! sed hunc prostravit
      Cito serpens callidus.
    Propter quod plebs procreata   4
    Succedit[1]⟨et⟩ condempnata;
    Sed sanavit sauciata
      Princeps penis pallidus.
    Hic, de luto qui nos lavit,   5
    Sibi ser(vum su)blevávit,
    Hunc patronu(m) publicavit
      Huius habitaculi.
    Nomen huius herimite   6
    Est Robertus, recte vite;
    Hic levavit sine lite
      Tronum tabernaculi.
    Pius pugill perbeatus,   7
    Eboraco procreatus,
    Est Robertus ac vocatus,
      Natus ex nobilibus.
    Nomen[2] Tok Flos patet patris,   8
    Sed Simima sue matris,
    Et Walterus fuit fratris,
      Maior factus civibus.
f. 1ᵛ   Hic adultus mansuetus   9
    Fuit, factisque facetus
    Pulcris, puris ac repletus
      Ornamentis morum,

[1] Succedat.   [2] Domen.

Appendix C

Pius, prudens ac perfectus,   10
Et a plebe predelectus,
Factis fedis nec infectus
   Fuit viciorum;
Deo dignus ac devotus,   11
Lacrimarum lacte lotus,
In tranquillitate totus
   Habitavit herimo.
Conditorem contemplatur,   12
Nichill sibi denegatur,
Dum hic Deum deprecatur
   Sono saluberimo.
Domus dapis declinavit,   13
Knaresburgo festinavit,
Ibi carnem conculcavit
   Miris ⟨ab⟩stinenciis.
Adherebat heremite   14
Valde virtuose vite,
Latitanti sine lite,
   Presso penitenciis.
Inspiratus sponte sprevit   15
Voluptatis facta; flevit,
Et sub rupe requievit
   Fretus in foramine.
Hic Robertus residebat,   16
Dum prodire proponebat
Herimata quem habebat
   Secum pro solamine.

f. 2   Sic vir valde veneratus,   17
Lectis libris litteratus,
Sibi sumpsit sublimatus
   Statum subdiaconi.
Tunc ad fratrem festinavit,   18
Qui conversus habitavit,
Here⟨s⟩ ubi hympnizavit
   Novi Monasterii.
Approbavit hic beatus   19
Meros mores monachatus,
Quibus fuit informatus
   Sequi solitaria.
Ad matronam tunc migravit;   20
A qua quidem impetravit
Vite victum. Nec negavit
   Dare necessaria,
Concedebat hec capellam   21

Appendix C

 Hilde Sacre, sibi cellam;
Non pavebant ob puellam
 Fures hanc effodere.
In Robertum irrumpebantt,   22
Panem, potum rapiebantt,
Ac ab eo aufferebantt
 Res ac raptas rodere.
Hinc ad Spofford villam venit,   23
Antrum altum sic invenit,
Non elatum laude lenit
 Plenitudo populi.
Qua de causa declinavit   24
Hedeley, ubi habitavit;
Se ad visum cucullavit
 Intuentis oculi.

f. 2ᵛ   Una veste iam ve⟨s⟩tatus,   25
Est a reis reprobatus;
Sustinebat non iratus
 Illatas iniurias.
Ad capellam Hilde Sacre   26
Est reversus habitare,
Mallens fures infestare
 Quam pristas penurias.
Dum Robertus dormitavit,   27
Mesta mater se monstravit
Penis pressam, ac oravit
 Prolem pro se petere.
Item ipso dormitante   28
Apperebat hic ut ante,
Ac reatum revelante
 Nill illatum ledere.
Knaresburgo remeavit   29
Homo hic, ac habitavit
In capella, quam fundavit
 Quis quondam Egidii.
Ibi modo meliori   30
Serviebat sanctiori,
Rupe raptus, redemptori,
 Expers omnis vicii.
Hinc Willelmus, vir vocatus,   31
Facto fumo fit gravatus,
Est a servis scicitatus;
 Sonant solitarium.
Eius ut audivit actus,   32
Frendit, frenit, furens factus

Appendix C

  Iuramentum, ira tactus,
   Tulit temerarium.
  Dicens domum ut deleret,   33
  In spelunca hic ut speret
  Feras ferre, ac has feret,
   Latet in latibulo.
  Tunc Robertus, his auditis,   34
  Ait autem satis scitis,
  'Non movebit me invitis
   Lupus de hoc lapide.
  Velit nolit, sine fine,   35
  Hic manebo; sue mine
  Me non move⟨n⟩t quam de crine
   Cadit qui de capite.'
  Sed in nocte sic sequente,   36
  Dicto duce dormiente,
  Irruentes tres repente
   Currunt cum curriculo.
  Gaudet. Currus fit formidans;   37
  Adest unus palma portans
  Duas clavas, ac exhortans
   Ipsum unam capere.
  Horret homo, tremit totus,   38
  Metuebat, mente motus;
  Evanescunt, ut ignotus,
   Qui ruebant rapere.
  Sic Willelmus, versus visu,   39
  Nova narrans nutu nisu,
  Ad Robertum sine visu
   Currit cum comitibus.
  In caverna hic curvatus,   40
  De delicto condempnatus,
  Terram dedit dominatus
   Huic ac hospitibus.
  Victus dedit duodenis   41
  Elimosinam egenis,
  Refocillans hos in cenis
   Suis cum cibariis;
  Quos Robertus roboravit,   42
  Claudos, curvos hic curavit,
  Surdos, secos saturavit
   Notis necessariis.
  Venit frater hic Walterus,   43
  Eboraci maior merus,
  Pius preses ac procerus

Appendix C

Tunc qui statum tenuit,
Ut a rupe removeret 44
Hunc Robertum ut haberett
Mansionem, qua manerett;
 Sed redire renuit.
Cernens eius sanitatem, 45
Solam sic stabilitatem,
Nil curans hereditatem,
 Manu tunc artificis
Hanc construxit sibi cellam, 46
Sancte Crucisque capellam
Innovavit ac novellam
 Multis beneficiis.
Die domnus deambulavit, 47
Yvonem sibi sociavit,
Viva voce hunc vocavit,
 'Me per mores sequere.'
Est secutus vite vias, 48
Porrigendo preces pias;
Sublevavit per sophias
 Cor contritum ethere.
Rixat Yvo cum Roberto, 49
Sic discessit de deserto,
Casu cadit in incerto;
 Ramo terit tibiam.
Dolet Yvo; adest iste 50
Temperando totum triste,
'Gradum tuum cito siste;
 Postpone perfidiam.
Migra, miser, mansioni; 51
Vacca contemplacioni;
Dudum dominacioni
 Prece placuisti.'
Sic saluti resolutus, 52
Est pastorem prosecutus,
Attemptatus erat tutus
 Caritate Cristi.
Eboracum nudus nive 53
Pedes pergit processive;
Sanguis stillans successive
 Tinxit territorium.[1]
Hinc latrones inprovisi, 54
Quinque quidem sunt occisi,
Qui frangentes erant visi

[1] territoritorium.

Appendix C

Eius oratorium.
Dum hic semel supplicavit 55
Dictis demon derogavit,
Quem tunc foras effugavit
    Benedicto baculo.
Rudis rursum irruebat, 56
Quasi puer apperebat,
'Vade, miser,' hic dicebat,
    'Ab hoc habitaculo.'
Quondam hic crudelis cocus, 57
Ut concremaretur locus,
In stramento ferox[1] focus
    Datur a diabolo.
Creb⟨r⟩o currit hic crudelis 58
Ad capellam cum cautelis,
Ut sic fiat infidelis
    Raptus reciaculo.
Rex cavernam concupivit 59
Contemplari; in hanc ivit.
Non assurgit, quamvis scivit
    Hunc, prostratus precibus.

f. 4ᵛ   Quidam sibi asserebat 60
An hunc virum agnoscebat;
Sic Robertus respondebat
    Cunctis in conspectibus:
'Hic Iohannes est illustris, 61
Pronus princeps, rex prelustris,'
Cui comes de collustris
    Ait inter alias:
'Roga regem ut de rebus 62
Tibi donet his[2] diebus,
Utpote de speciebus
    His vigere valeas.'
Tunc Robertus referenti, 63
'Michi, Cristum cupienti,
Nichill auri vell argenti
    Deest transitoriis.'
Increpatus ab Yvone 64
Est Robertus racione,
Quia de possessione
    Nill tunc petit posteris.
Hinc ad regem reversurus 65
Est Robertus, rogaturus
Pressis et hoc possessurus

---

[1] ferax.   [2] donec hic.

Appendix C

Piis in perpetuum.
Carucatam conferebat 66
Comitatus, quam colebat,
Boscum, boves ac prebebat
    Egenis in subsedium.
Spicam sumpsit indilate 67
Sonans sic suavitate,
'Potes, princeps, potestate
    Hanc creare nichilo?'
Negat ille; hii ridebant, 68
Ac Robertum deludebant.
'Hic est stultus,' asserebant,
    'Clausus in cubiculo.'

f. 5

At Robertus rursum ivit, 69
Vaccam unam expetivit;
Comes quidem accersivit
    Et libenter tribuit.
Hic ut miser mendicavit 70
Quibus sibi sociavit,
Pane, potu, prece pavit,
    Ac sanare studuit.
Dux donabat tunc Roberto 71
Vaccam feram in deserto,
Quam deduxit in aperto
    Mansuetam moribus.
Domum duxit; dicte gentes 72
Obstupescunt intuentes;
Horum monebantur mentes
    In interio⟨ri⟩bus.
Ait unus, 'Vadam vere 73
Vaccam vestram rehabere
Apta arte,' sed silere
    Comes hunc consuluit.
Finxit fautor falsitatem 74
Pretendendo paupertatem,
Petit propter pietatem
    Vaccam; et hanc tribuit.
Hanc fautore sic fugante, 75
Claudicavit post ut ante,
Sic pro vacca vindicante
    Deo risus rediit.
Clamat miser, 'Meserere, 76
O Roberte, intuere
Michi; preco indulgere,'
    Et hoc cito subiit.

Appendix C

Non sunt vana hec, sed vera; 77
Obedivit sibi fera,
Avis, cervus, ut scincera
    Protestatur pagina.
Sepe cervi irruerunt, 78
Seminatum secuerunt,
Tales terram turbant, terunt,
    Totam preter stramina.
Mas hic mitis et modestus, 79
Fatis feris sic infestus,
Miro modo ut molestus,
    Est conquestus comiti.
Cui comes functus fraude, 80
'Cultor Cristi, cervos claude
Ut mitescant tua laude
    Dicti sic indomiti.'
Campo currit, ac clausure 81
Cervos tollit de tellure;
Concernentes creature
    Cuncte canunt carmine.
Clausis cervis per hunc vatem, 82
Remeavit ad magnatem,
'Propter prodigalitatem
    Solve captos crimine.'
Dum propheta hec affatur 83
Corde comes consternatur,
Parte mundus meriatur
    Communiri meritis.
'Propter vias vite veras 84
Scanctitatesque (?) scinceras,
Has confirmo tibi feras
    Attractandis aratris.'
Iste sanctus seminavit 85
Semen suum, ac aravit
Cervis, quos concopulavit
    Lassos in laboribus.
Isdem victum adquesivit; 86
Mansuete obedivit
Sibi cervus; sic vir vivit
    Hympnis ac honoribus.
Rector ruit tunc Roberto, 87
'Solve,' sonans, 'de asserto
Decimales; non differto
    Garbas, herbas reddere.'
Hoc distincte denegavit; 88

Appendix C

Cum rectore replicavit,
'Nullas reddam,' resonavit,
'Parce, precor, petere.'
Dictus dixit, 'Certe dabis,   89
Velis nolis, decimabis
De frumento et de fabis,
Fenum sive fuerit.'
Prophetavit paginista,   90
'Lingua tua, iam lanista,
Lanietur propter ista.'
Sic vir pestem peperit.
Est Brianus benedictus   91
A Roberto, non relictus;
Prophetavit hec predictus
Sibi in itenere,
'Mero motu iam meabis,   92
Nec ad domum declinabis;
Corpus cadet casu cladis
Coopertum cinere.'
Prophetavit cum processu   93
Tunc Robertus de recessu,
It⟨e⟩m idem de ingressu
Et de grandi gloria.
'Mundum mestum non amavi,   94
Celum semper suspiravi,
Deum non[1] desideravi
Mentis cum memoria.'
Dixit, 'Dum hic in condensis   95
Sum sepultus cum incensis,
Fortitudo Fontanensis
Corpus ruent rapere.
Hic quiescam sine fine;   96
Reddo regi ac regine,
Trinitati uni trine
Comendatum capere.'
Tunc 'In manus' memoravit,   97
Creatori commendavit,
Crucis signo se signavit
Et emisit spiritum.
Astat chorus angelorum,   98
Sumpto cetu ceterorum,
Pios plausos ad polorum
Perducebantt inclitum.
De decessu audientes,   99

---

[1] Read tam?

Appendix C

Festinabant Fontanenses,
Corpus credunt capientes
  Ferre cum preconio.
Sed resistunt cum rigore   100
Armatorum multi more,
Recedentes cum rumore
  Condolentes domino.
Mors cum crevit manifesta,   101
Mansit multitudo mesta;
Fletus factus in foresta
  Est multorum milium.
Famulorum fuit factus   102
Fortis fletus, fide fractus;
Agitantur propter actus
  Morum mirabilium.
Ruunt iam religiosi,   103
Pauper, potens, preciosi,
Pro defuncto dolorosi,
  Virgo, vir et vidue.

f. 7
'Quis a lupis liberabit?   104
Quis pro servis supplicabit?
Quis sermone nos cibabit?'
  Sonant sic assidue.
Yvo, cum ingenti cura,   105
Preparavit, inter plura,
Secum cuncta creatura
  Corpus tumbe tradere.
Choro coram concinente,[1]   106
Comita⟨t⟩u[2] consequente,
Tumba tecta, tunc repente
  Retro vertunt vadere.
Hic patronus pietatis   107
Coram trono trinitatis
Obstet; oret pro peccatis,
  Precis patrociniis,
Ut mundemur in hoc mundo,   108
Et saluemur in secundo;
Nos perducat de profundo
  Celi sanctis veneis.
Votis, voce universi   109
Confluebantt, tunc conversi
Ad sepulcrum ut submersi
  In inferni fluctibus;
Ut iniqui et inepti   110

---

[1] concumente.   [2] Comitaui.

Appendix C

A reatu sunt erepti;
Sic salutem sunt adepti
Lacrimarum luctibus.
Currit claudus, surdus, cecus,   111
Totum dante Deo decus,
Quia prece pastor, pecus
Prosperantur prestita.
Multi lesique leprosi,   112
Luna lapsi, furiosi,
Huius prece preciosi
Emundantur mistica.

f. 7ᵛ   Tumba tamen protestatur,   113
Ubi vir hic veneratur,
Hec non falsa, ut affatur
Preciosa pagina.
Licet non canonicatur,   114
Adhuc autem operatur
Per hunc pater cum precatur,
Plura beneficia.
Hympnus, honor heremite,   115
Iam Roberto recte vite;
Lator legis elargite
Salus et solamen.
Hec ut perste⟨n⟩t atque plura,   116
Cuncta canat creatura,
Maior, minor mente pura,
Singillatim 'Amen'.   Explicit.

APPENDIX D

The following Latin account of the foundation of the Order of the Holy Trinity (*HT*.) is contained in the British Museum Manuscript, Egerton 3143, ff. 7ᵛ–10ʳ.

f. 7ᵛ   De innovatione Ordinis Sancte Trinitatis.

Hic et fundo digni ducis
Locus, ut lucerna lucis,
Signo sancte Cristi crucis,
Ut affatur famine.
Causa celle sit scincere   2
Plasmatori complacere,
Et in cella exercere
Almos actus anime.
Locus laudis hic levatur   3
In quo Cristus collaudatur,

Appendix D

  Horis, hympnis honoratur
   Hic cum sanctis singulis.
  In hoc ordo Trinitatis   4
  Exaltatur cum beatis;
  Templum est tranquillitatis
   Curis cum continuis.
  Fratres ferunt crucem Cristi,   5
  Meditando mente tristi
  Redemptorem, per quem isti
   Sunt salvati sanguine.
  Crux creatur in cruore,   6
  Bene blodiali more,
  Rubicundo cum colore,
   Deferenda pectore.
  Conditoris tunc cruorem,   7
  Fusum nostrum ob amorem
  Ad purgandum p⟨er⟩ (?) pecorem,
   Representant rubeus.
  Per undam hanc qua sumus toti,   8
  Labe lapsi, modo loti
  Poli plaususque promoti,
   Signat color blodius.
  Sed hec crux est lateralis,   9
  Que mundavit nos a malis,
  Quia plaga pectoralis
   Plasmatoris extitit.
  Ordo, fratres hanc ferentes   10
  Intus, infra, extra gentes,
  Cristi crucis recolentes,
   Sitis quam hic subiit.
  Vestra vestis venerata,   11
  In colore candidata,
  Est hec causa designata
   Honorato homini—
  Alba, quia angelorum   12
  Vestes erant vi valorum
  Cura cum servatur horum
   Sic sepulcrum domini;
  Vestimenti ac albedo   13
  Signat castitatem, credo,
  Quia in vestitu fedo
   Memoratur macula.
  Deturpator perit pestis;   14
  Puritatem patet vestis,
  Intus, extra, michi testis

Appendix D

    Est Johannes aquila.
Ordo noster paupertatis   15
Est hic ordo Trinitatis,
Hoc est pro triplicitatis
    Nota necessaria.
Hic ordo, cura caritatis,   16
De possessis propetratis,
Ac de cunctis congregatis,
    Mittunt ultra maria
Perigrinis et egenis,   17
Pressis paganorum penis,
Sine pietate plenis,
    Redimendis milibus;
Sunt eorum infiniti   18
Carcerati, compediti,
Penis pressis prepediti;
    Sedent in similibus,
Fletu freti, flagellati,   19
Cum cathenis colligati;
Omnes sunt angustiati
    Penis in pregravibus.
Multi manent macerati,   20
Operati, onerati,
Ac cum bobis attractati,
    Custoditi clavibus.
Spine punctis perforati,   21
Rusticis rediculati,
Plures penas iam sunt pati,
    Fari quam sufficimus.
Pro his quidem redimendis,   22
Et ad domos reducendis,
Ac a reis rehabendis,
    Satis summam solvimus.
Trina parte facultatum   23
Nobis manu iam magnatum
Transmissarum paganatum
    Constudemus solvere;
Ac bonorum parte bina   24
In hac vita vis divina
Servos cibat de coquina,
    Sic ut possint vivere.
Sic cibamur in hac vita   25
Facultate tripartita
Trinitatis; tantum ita
    Est referta regula.

Appendix D

Omnes ergo obedite	26
Huic venerate vite;	
Vobis dicet, 'Tunc venite'	
Qui salvabit secula.	
Ordo Sancte Trinitatis	27
Flos est fraternitatis,	
Qui ut sol serenitatis	
Prefulgebit fratribus.	
Miti micat hic ministro,	28
Ministrante quam magistro.	
Racionem reddet Cristo	
Hic[1] cum piis precibus.	
Hic minister memoratur,	29
Qui ut servus dominatur,	
Ut prelatus preferatur,	
Decet ut pastoribus.	
In scriptura salutari	30
Deus est dignatus fari,	
'Huc non veni ministrari,	
Sed ministrare moribus.'	
Ordo sanus est inceptus,	31
Per quem reus est ereptus,	
Contradicens est deceptus,	
Ut patescit pagina.	
Hic per vias heremitas,	32
Virtuose redimitas,	
Eligerunt sibi vitas,	
Quis salvetur anima.[2]	
Quondam quidem heremite	33
Pro securitate vite,	
Latitantes sine lite,	
Habitantes herimo,	
Pio pape prodierunt,	34
Ut perfecti pecierunt;	
Hoc concessum est qui querunt	
Statu pro scincerimo.	
Sed confestim celebrante	35
Papa, plebe perastante,	
Celi rege revelante,	
Candidata cecidit	
Cruce consignata vestis,	36
Quam (est scriptor michi testis)	
Mansuetis ac modestis,	
Pius papa prebuit.	

f. 9v (at line 30)

[1] Hii.   [2] quis quibus *at the side.*

Appendix D

  Dicti duo tunc periti,   37
  Alba veste sic vestiti,
  Voluntate non inviti,
   Innovabant ordinem.
  Ordo huius honestatis,   38
  Patronatu Trinitatis,
  Cristi cruce cum signatis,
   Sic cepit originem.

f. 10 Dudum dicti adimatis,   39
  Cunctis cruce consignatis,
  Cunctos concaptivitatis
   Clausos in carce⟨ri⟩bus
  Paganorum redimerunt,   40
  A rigore rapuerunt,
  Panem, potum prebuerunt,
   Pressis pre verberibus.
  Huic omnes obligati   41
  Sunt professi Trinitati;
  Si non curent cruciati,
   Erunt domo demonis.
  Facultatis[1] trina parte   42
  Persolverunt tunc aparte,
  Fati fratres sicut carte
   Attestantes ordinis.
  Modo, fratres, valeatis;   43
  Commendamus vos beatis,
  Mundi regnum[2] recolatis;
   Transit sicut sompnia.
  Ergo sumpti ab hoc solo,   44
  Complaudentes sitis polo
  Deum mecum, quem hic colo;
   'Amen' dicant omnia.

   Explicit.

[1] Facultate.   [2] rignum.

The manufacturer's authorised representative in the EU for product safety is Oxford University Press España S.A. of El Parque Empresarial San Fernando de Henares, Avenida de Castilla, 2 - 28830 Madrid (www.oup.es/en or product.safety@oup.com). OUP España S.A. also acts as importer into Spain of products made by the manufacturer.

Printed and bound by CPI Group (UK) Ltd, Croydon, CR0 4YY

02/04/2026

02083149-0020